Copyright 20..

ISBN-13 978-0-692-03159-9

Published by

ISBN 978-0-692-03159-9 $12.50

51250

Keywords: Kansas, Underground railroad, Slaves

Please contact the author with any questions or comments regarding contents of this publication or to purchase a copy of the book.

Karen Scroggins
311 W. Walnut St.
Junction City, Ks 66441
Kscroggins31@yahoo.com

Acknowledgements

The Printery, Sherry Kent for the recipes, Dorothy Bramlage Public Library that helped in the editing this text. Tanya Collins for technical support. Joe Fagan, Kathleen Harris, Bonnie McClintock, Morris County Historical Society, Judy Sweet-genealogist, Marcia Schulely of Riley County Historical Society, Chapman Rural Study-Kansas State University, Mr. Tom Moxley, Jim Sharp, Last but not least to all family- Mrs. Linda Gadson-Virgil Campbell, Mrs. Shirley Jones, Christopher and Kurtis Broadnax, Dennis Campbell, D.J. Barrnett and friends for their help and encouragement all the way.

Whatever you put your hand to do,
do your BEST and you will be the
BEST

Rosetta Ragland

Table of Contents

Preface

Acknowledgements

Preface

Karen (Campbell) Scroggins is a Kansas native, born in Council Grove, Kansas. She was raised in Russell, Kansas, and Bob Dole was her neighbor. Being the third in a family of five, she was taught to be self-supporting and a productive member of the community. There were no unimportant jobs, whether it was washing dishes or putting them away since without clean dishes people cannot eat. Karen was taught, "Do your best at whatever the job may be."

Although Karen's mother did not originally finish high school, she encouraged her children to finish their education. Later, Karen's mother finished school and became a nurse. Karen was unable to finish school, but she got her GED. Shortly after a family crisis, she entered Manhattan Vocational School in the Dietary Technician program and before graduating entered Kansas State University. In 1993, she received her BS in Food and Nutrition with a secondary degree in Gerontology, the study of aging. In 1993, she received her Master's Degree in Adult and Continuing Education from Kansas State University.

In more recent year, Karen visited her great, great grandmother until she went home to be Jesus. Karen believes we all can learn from seniors. Her grandmother, Tinnie (Rosetta Tennessee Ragland), told her stories that her mother told her, and Karen began to research her family history. This book is the result of that research.

Tinnie (Rosetta Tennessee Ragland)

How it all began: Nancy Gupton's Story

Grew was the blacksmith and driver for his master, Mr. Gupton, at the Crossing Road Plantation in Tennessee. They would come to our plantation, Belle Meade Plantation, also in Tennessee, when they wanted to buy slaves. My mother and I worked in the Big House on our plantation. Most slaves that worked in the House were less likely to be sold, but Grew was afraid of me being sold because he and I were secretly married. I was also expecting our first child, but I did not tell Grew.

Life for slaves could be very hard. If slaves tried to run away they would be whipped or would have bells put on their heads.

Woman wearing bells and horns to prevent her from running away

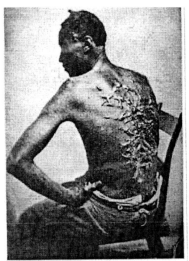

Scars of whipped slave. This famous 1863 photo was distributed by abolitionists to illustrate what they saw as the barbarism of Southern society.[24] That the victim likely suffered from keloid, according to Kathleen Collins,[25], making the scars more prominent and extensive, does not detract from the savagery of flogging.

One day Grew told us that we were going to be sold to Mr. Gupton, his master from Cross Road Plantation. We often talked about following the North Star and getting on the Underground Railroad that would take us to Canada and freedom. I would often dream of being free and I believed my children would be born free, but I was afraid to leave because I had never been away from my family. That night I had a dream about freedom. I was talking to God, and I saw a house at the top of a hill with a long, long driveway, animal buildings, land as far as I could see, a dove, and my children playing—just running and running.

Grew's dream about going to Canada seemed to be becoming real as he packed his tools. It had been raining for two days, and nobody was working in the fields. Grew asked me to pack dried meats and onions. I did not like to eat raw onions, only cooked ones, but I packed them anyway.

We left in the rain. I prayed I would not get sick, but I got so sick that I thought I would die. Then I would remember my dream, and we kept going toward the North Star. Sometimes it was cloudy, so we had to depend on what we knew. We knew the moss grew on the north side of the trees.

Sometimes we heard dogs coming, and we knew we had to chop up the onions and rub them all over our bodies to keep the dogs away. It made me sick, but I knew I had to do it to stay safe. I was good at finding things to eat.

SUNNY KANSAS!

Land of John Brown
Men, Women & Children

Promised to Everyone
$500, 40 acres and a mule
Apples as big as grapefruit

"Complete equality"
Literary & Business Academy
Dunlap Academy and Mission School
Two local agencies:
The Presbyterian Church and the Freedmen's
Aid Association of Dunlap Supported
Settlement

We came to a point that our plans needed to change because I was with child. The pain in my back was hurting me so bad that I could barely walk. We were going to have to find somewhere to go other than Canada. The next thing I knew, Grew had brought home a poster about sunny Kansas: Land of John Brown. The poster promised to every free man, $500, 40 acres and a mule. There were to be first-class hotels, apples as big as grapefruit, complete equality, a 12 X 16 foot cabin, livestock, 2 horses, a cow and seven hogs.

We now knew we had to get to the Neosho River, through forests and swamps, to get to The Underground Railroad, which was a network of hiding places established by abolitionists where runaway slaves could eat, rest and get a change of clothes on their trip northward.

Secret Codes of the Undergrond Railroad of Kansas said that if there was a Quilt on the wash line it was a safe house for the slaves on their way to freedom.

Secret Codes of the Underground Railroad of Kansas said that if there was two candles in the window this was DANGER to keep going on their way to freedom.

Secret Codes of the Underground Railroad of
Kansas said that if there was one candle in
the window this was a friendly place where
the slaves could be on their way to freedom.

Secret Codes of the Underground Railroad of
Kansas had instructions given to the slaves in
the songs they sang along the way on their
way to freedom, they would listen for
directions on when to get ready to move and
where was sage on their way to freedom.

February of 1880, more than 900 black families from Mississippi reaching the route to Kansas. Some black migrants sought "conductors" to make travel arrangements for them. These conductors would often ask for money but then not show up at the appointed departure time, leaving migrants

stranded at the stations.

(Picture Emigrants Traveling to Kansas) Refugees on Levee, 1879. Carroll's Art Gallery. Photomural from gelatin Prints and Photographs Division (105) prints and Photographs Division.

Individuals or whole familes of African-Americans passing northward through St. Louis was not a novel sight. But this was a new situation. As time passed it became clear the stories the first migrants had told to Mr. Tandy were all too true. From all the South, but especially from Texas, Louisiana, and Mississippi, many thousands of black ex-slaves were surging North.

Nothing seemed to stop the new migrants. Neither bitter cold, the new strange surroundings, the threats of reprisals, or promises of better treatment had an effect. Half-starved, they arrived in St. Louis, Topeka, and Kansas City. and fanned out to Kansas, Indiana, and Ohio. Through the misery and despair, the fear and distrust, there could be detected a spirit of hope.

The yearnings of those moving northward were captured more than forty years later by a black poet. She cried out in common dialect of that time:

Huh! De wurl" ain't flat
An' de wart' ain't roun'
Jes' one long strip
Hangin' up and down.
Since Norf is up
An' Souf is down
An' Hebben is up,
I'm upward boun'
We traveled down the river and landed in Council
Grove. From there we went through a tunnel under
a big house. At nightfall we were loaded into a
wagon and taken to White City, then to Dunlap,
Kansas.

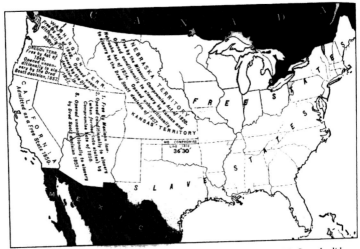

Map showing the slave states (gray) and free states (white) as of 1857. Canada did
not allow slavery.

Coming to Kansas

Kansas State Capitol

The Tragic Prelude, segment of the encompassing murals by John Steuart Curry, Kansas Statehouse in Topeka. Among the finest public art in the country is John Brown leading antislavery forces in Kansas Territory. The tornado represents the warfare that swept the land.

Kansas State Capitol Tour Center
10th & Jackson
Topeka, KS 66612
785-296-3966
capitol@kshs.org

The Man Responsible for Bringing Us to Dunlap, a Moses Named Singleton

Benjamin Singleton, a Kansas Portrait

He was born a slave in 1809, but after 37 years of bondage Benjamin Singleton escaped to freedom. He made Detroit his home and operated a secret boarding house for other escaped slaves. Following emancipation, Singleton returned to his native Tennessee.

After the Civil War, African Americans in the South enjoyed the rights and privileges of American citizenship. But when the federal troops were removed, theirs right were no longer secure. The Ku Klux Klan emerged to strike terror and death to Blacks who refused to submit to their will. A sharecropping system virtually re-enslaved Black tenant farmers.

Because Kansas was famous for John Brown's efforts and its struggle against slavery, Singleton considered the state a New Canaan, and he, like a "Black Moses," would lead his people to the promised land. Singleton traveled through the South organizing parties to colonize in Kansas. In 1873 nearly 300 Blacks followed him to Cherokee County and founded "Singleton's Colony." Others settled in Wyandotte, in Topeka's Tennessee Town, and in Dunlap Colony near present Emporia.

Singleton advocated the organized colonization of Blacks in communities like Nicodemus, first settled in 1877. Between

1879 and 1881, however, the organized Movement gave way to an "Exodus" in which tens of thousands of oppressed and impoverished Southern Blacks fled to Kansas and other Northern states. Many came unprepared but most who remained ultimately improved the quality of their lives and made important contributions to the state and the communities in which they lived.

Known affectionately as "Pap," Benjamin Singleton died in 1892. Through his last years he took great comfort and pride in the role in played as "Father of the Negro Exodus" (http://www.kshs.org/portraits/singleton_benjamin.htm).

Pap Singleton, as it turns out, was buried in Kansas City, Missouri, at the Union Cemetery. Genealogists Sweet and Schuley found the grave, according to journalist Mike Hendricks (reachable at mhendricks@kcstar.com).

Black migrants Singleton brought to Kansas were settled on the land. The problem with many of the migrants was that they had run out of money getting themselves and their families settled in Kansas. Some of them would have to find the financial resources necessary to make down payments and the six annual installments. Of the first 300 families that Singleton brought to Dunlap to purchase land, some fifty families had run out of resources. In 1878, Benjamin Singleton, being honest and trustworthy, served as a benefactor who helped them organize a call for outside financial help.

The following are the number of members he helped– giving the number in family and the number of acres each.

Name	Number in Family	Number Acres
John Davis	2	80
John Mathew	2	40
Solomon West	6	40
George Wade	3	140
Wm. Acker	4	80
Moses Chipley	2	40
A. Powers	4	40
Jeff Willis	8	40
Ren Morris	3	40
Warner Washington	4	40
Harl Henderson	7	40
Elisha Zanlett	6	40
Prince Gold	9	160
Grew Gupton	3	80
Armstead Robinson	3	40
Henry Carter	4	40
Andrew Pleasant	4	40
Dewy Baily	6	160
Thomas Talbert	3	40
Lewis Thompson	2	40
A.W. Croney	8	40
Wm. Shrout	5	0
Capt. Pierce	3	40
Jos. Bridges	6	100
Ray Bridges	5	100
Mike Cooper	7	80
Clev Sutter	7	40
Green Myers	4	40
Glenn Dibble	4	40
Ellis McMay	3	80
Waria Ross	3	40
C. Mathews	2	80
Richard Crutaher	4	40
Leiors Galtie	6	80

Total Families	34	
Total Family Members	149	
Total Acres	2060	

W.S. Miller, Secretary

Dunlap Kaw (*KSHS Singleton Papers*)

The Colony At Dunlap

Dunlap, Kansas
August 9, 1878

At a special meeting of the colored people of Dunlap and vicinity, E. Horn was elected Chairman and W.S. Miller secretary. Prayer was offered by Elisha Bartlett.

The object of the meeting being stated by the chairman—which was the subject of Colonization– after discussing the matter thoroughly, agreed upon Colonization. Benjamin Singleton was appointed agent to procure same to be known as the Singleton Colony by authority of a charter issued on 25 day of June and from the office of Secretary of State. The following officers were elected for the present— Andrew Pleasant Vice-President, W.S. Miller, Corresponding Secretary, Joseph Ray, Treasurer, David Smith, Marshall.

In spring of 1878, Singleton redirected his efforts to parts of Kansas where land was available through the 1862 Homestead Act and successfully established a colony at Dunlap in Morris County (central Kansas). The famous Nicodemus Colony in Graham County was established in the summer of 1877, which had nothing to do with Dunlap.

Dunlap was the second largest black settlement in Kansas.

The town of Dunlap had a strong beginning, as told to me by Mr. Barnard's Grandfather who was one of the city fathers and desired to have Dunlap on the hill just west of Dunlap's present site. During a night in 1877, Joseph Dunlap and a companion, Mr. Guthria, took a team of horses and plow and marked the present site of Dunlap. Negroes had already been living in the area. Indians had lived there. It seemed to be a good spot to build a town. An early settler built his house at least one half mile from downtown Dunlap visualizing that Main Street would touch his house during his lifetime.

He was an Indian Trader and is believed to be the first white settler in the area and the second farmer in the Dunlap area. (Paper of Mrs. A. N. Parish)

Joseph Dunlap is shown seated by his wife and surrounded by family and friends. He is responsible for incorporating the village in 1874. Dunlap had risen to prominence as a trader on the Kansa Indian Reservation and the Sante Fe Trail near Council Grove. Originally hailed from Marion, Kansas--family emigrat ed from Scotland

Before Dunlap became a colony, Negroes had

already been living in the area.

*Charles and Jennie Singleton Harness- the first
Black family in the Reservation area (Historic
photo from art & Gen Harness)*

Mother   *Father*
Anna M.   *London A.*
June 22,1908   *Nov. 12, 1906*

Dec. 20, 1986   *Apr. 27, 1993*

Actually, Dunlap unofficially started with a Lady's dream. She was from Chicago. She bought 160 acres of the Kaw's land and built houses 14 by 16 feet. She sold them cheaply or gave the land 10 to 20 acre parcels to Negroes who migrated from the South. The lady built an academy to help educate the Black. This all began in 1868, lasting until 1873.

The academy was originally designated for "colored" students only, but eventually both black and white Students attended.

(Historic Photo – Fern Gayen)

*Dunlap Academy and Mission School (1881-1889)-
Both black and white attended.*

KANSAS COLORED

LITERARY & BUSINESS

ACADEMY

Dunlap, Morris County, Kansas.

Republican Print, Council Grove, Ks.

*Kansas Colored
Literary &Business
ACADEMY
Dunlap, Morris County, Kansas
Republican Print, Council Grove, Ks*

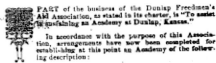

Part of the business of the Dunlap Freedmen's Aid Association, as Stated in its charter is "To assist in sustaining an Academy at Dunlap, Kansas."

In accordance with the purpose of this Association, arrangements have now been completed for establishing at this point an Academy of the following description:

I. TERMS OF ADMISSION
CANDIDATES for admission to the first class of the course must pass a creditable examination in

Reading, Writing, Arithmetic to Percentage,
Elements of Language, and Elements of Geography.

Those who possess more extensive qualifications
may enter higher classes.

II. *COURSES OF INSTRUCTION*
   1. *LITERARY AND NORMAL COURSE*
   2. *BUSINESS COURSE*

The First Course comprises the work of three years,
and is intended to lead students to the grade
required for entrance to the Freshman Class of the
State University. In this course thorough Normal
instruction will be given to such as desire to qualify
themselves for teaching. To aid in this department
of training, our students will have an immense
advantage in a Practices School of over one
hundred pupils, in which the Principles and
methods of primary instruction will be verified
before their eyes.

The Second Course of Instruction comprises the
work of two years, and is intended to it students,
both male and female, for making the most of
themselves through the means of the different
occupations of life. It will qualify young men and
women for commercial clerkships and drill them in
the principles and practice of economy. Students
taking this course will be carefully instructed in
Business Law, both Moral and Civil.

III. SCHOOL CALENDAR
THE school year commences on the second Monday of September.

The year is divided into three terms, of twelve weeks each. Short vacations about January 1st and April 1st.

advantage in a Practice School of over one hundred pupils, in which all the principles and methods of primary instruction will be verified before their eyes.

The Second Course of Instruction comprises the work of two years, and is intended to fit students, both male and female, for making the most of themselves through the means of the different occupations of life. It will qualify young men and women for commercial clerkships and drill them in the principles and practice of economy. Students taking this course will be carefully instructed in Business Law, both Moral and Civil.

⇒ III. ✦ SCHOOL ✦ CALENDAR. ✦

THE school year commences on the second Monday of September. The year is divided into three terms, of twelve weeks each. Short vacations about January 1st and April 1st.

⇥ IV. × Inducements × to × Attend × the + Colored × Academy at × Dunlap. ⇥

THE school is organized in the spirit of patriotism and charity.

2. The school is *free*. A contingent fee of Two Dollars a term is the entire charge to students.

3. We will endeavor to secure for our graduates paying positions as teachers or clerks. Business preserves education.

4. Vocal culture, both for oratory and music, a specialty.

IV. Inducements to Attend the Colored Academy at Dunlap
The school is organized in the spirit of patriotism and charity.

2. The school is free. A contingent fee of Two Dollars a term is the entire charge to students. 3. We will endeavor to secure for our graduates paying positions as teachers or clerks. Business preserves education. 4. Vocal culture, both for oratory and music, a specialty. A first-class instruction in vocal music.

5. An excellent new building, with comfortable rooms for students. Good boarding, Two Dollars and Fifty Cents per week, under care of teachers. Students board themselves at much lower rates.

6. Especial attention will be paid to Colored Preachers who may desire primary instruction, or to acquaint themselves with Church History or the Bible in the original.

7. The teachers will live for and with our students. Evil habits will cause expulsion.

8. Good apparatus for the help of the student. A large collection of Fossils, Minerals, and Insects for the use of students in class work.

9. We waste no time of student or teacher in useless instruction. Each student is fitted for his own work.

Now, Colored Citizens, consider this earnest proposal to educate you. A thousand friends await your response. Here you are offered the services of three experienced Christian teachers. Compare the cost of living in the "barbarism of ignorance" with the expense of securing a home, or boarding near this Free School where you may live lives of knowledge and influence among your own people.

"The school-master is abroad! I trust more to him armed with his primer, than I do to the soldier in full military array, for upholding and extending the liberties of his country."

Remember, this school is for Colored people only. Connected with it, is a Primary School and Sewing School for girls.

The first term of the Academy will open on Monday, December 5th, 1881.

Students admitted at any time.

For further information, address

ANDREW ATCHISON,

Principal.

to acquaint themselves with Church History or the Bible in the original.

7. The teachers will live for and with our students. Evil habits will cause expulsion.

8. Good apparatus for the help of the student. A large collection of Fossils, Minerals, and Insects for the use of students in class work.

9. We waste no time of student or teacher in useless instruction.

Each student is fitted for his own work.

Now, Colored Citizens, consider this earnest proposal to educate you. A thousand friends await your response. Here you are offered the services of three experienced Christian teachers. Compare the cost of living in the "barbarism of ignorance" with the expense of securing a home, or boarding near this Free School where you may live lives of knowledge and influence among your own people.

"The school-master is abroad! I trust more in him armed with his primer, than I do to the soldier in full military array, for upholding and excluding the liberties of the country."

Remember, this school id for Colored people only. Connected with it, is a Primary School and Sewing School for girls.

The first term of the Academy will open on Monday, December 5th 1861.

Students admitted at any time.
For further information, address
ANDREW ATCHISON,
Principal.

The mission School was supported by two local agencies: the Presbyterian Church and the Freedmen's Aid Association of Dunlap Supported Settlement.

There were two main cemeteries in Dunlap, one for blacks and one for whites. Many Civil War veterans were in both. The gravestones, made of limestone which crumbles easily, inferred that most of the Negroes were very poor. Our family's plot was in Moxely's pasture - Ragland Cemetery.

The rural schools were integrated, except for District 61, which was an all-Black school. (Board of Education/Morris County Register Deeds) The Dunlap High School was also integrated. In the early days when everyone had a cow for their milk supply, Dunlap had a Community Pasture. (Juanita/Ervin Eldred Interview 2006, Lifetime Dunlap Residents)

By 1915 the town had two hotels, one on Main Street and one near the depot. At that time Dunlap had a car dealership, with cars arriving by train, 3 grocery stores, 2 banks, 2 hardware stores, a lumberyard, a butcher shop, a shoe repair shop, a doctor's office, 5 churches, 2 blacksmiths, a horse and mule barn, 2 cream buying stations, 2 rural mail carriers, a depot, a post office and a Freedman's Academy.

This the first time Lillian Campbell saw her family graveyard in Tom Moxley's pasture. Mr. Moxley is Representative of the 68th District, Chase, Geary, and Morris Counties.

Tennessee, wife of K. Black, Sep 16, 1841-Dec 16, 1897
"Though grief it gives 'tis much the best to say Thy will be done"

One tomb identifies four separate graves. Back of grave is Phillis.

Phillis, wife of H.H. Harding, Nov 13, 1824-Mar 19, 1907
"Blessed are the pure in heart, for they shall see God—Matt 5:8"

Infant Daughter D.F.M. & F. Means—Died Oct 10, 1898

Sarah Bailey, wife of H.G. Bailey, Oct 14, 1848-May 23, 1907
"For as much as Christ hath suffered in the flesh arm yourselves likewise, for he that hath suffered in the flesh hath ceased from sin—1 Peter 4:1."

*Fred Thompson, Kansas, Bugler, 65 Pioneer Inf.,
March 29, 1921*

Mother Manda Patterson, Died Jan. 20, 1912

Marion 1840-1920, Harriet 1889-1994

Corpl Thos. Harding, Co. C, 14 USCL

DUNLAP (BLACK) CEMETERY
Which is located north (1/4 mile) of the other
Dunlap Cemetery….NE of city of Dunlap:
GAYDEN, SUMMERS, CURRY, PATTERSON ,
SMITH , LOWERY, McGILL,,
WARREN,ROBINSON, WRIGHT, HOWARD,
JACKSON, THOMPSON, FORD, BRIDGES,
TALLEY, THOMPSON, BROWN, HAYS,
RAGLAND, DAVIS, McRORY, RAMSBIRG,
ROVINSON, BELL, BLACK, GLEN, GAYDEN,
JONES, FULCHEM, HARNESS,

CUMMINGHAM, TURNER, McHENRY,
MORRIS, RAY, STEWART, PAYNE, MERRITT,
McCRORY, JOHNSON, GAYDEN, MURRAY,
GANSON, GERALD, BURKS, BLUE,
SUMMERS, HOWARD, MOSES, JERALDS,L
In 1869 Union Pacific Railroad put a track through,
but the train did not stop in Dunlap. The railroad ran
through Missouri, Kansas, and Texas and was
therefore called the MKT and nicknamed Katy. It
ran a double-daily passengers service to Emporia.
(Dunlap, KS "A Study of Its Rise and Its Decline;
by Don Ehrlich. - Dec. 9, 1971

In 1874, Leonard Still, a merchant in Dunlap
registered $8,000 worth of sales. Negroes and
Whites kept coming into the area. Most White
settlers seemed by from east-central United States.
The Neosho Valley Creamery reported $60,000
yearly gain by 1879. By the year 1880, Dunlap had
at least one doctor in the town.

Everything seemed to be going strong for Dunlap.

The oldest locomotive on the M-K-T Lines is Engine 787, which was built by the Baldwin Locomotive Works in 1886. The engine has long been relieved from active revenue service and is now the "Goat" at Parsons Roundhouse. In this capacity it does not perform the commonly accepted function of a "goat" in initiating novices into the railroad game but serves the very essential duty of "spotting" engines to permit access to parts undergoing repair. The engine is regularly operated by Engineer Jake Davis who takes a great deal of pride in riding the "Goat" Mr. Davis is also an "old timer" on the Katy Lines.

Engine 387 is the first M-K-T locomotive to have the Katy Emblem painted on the tender and the engine number on the cab below the window. This use of the Emblem adds a certain element of personality to the engine and is part of a program to improve the appearance of locomotives handling the famous Katy trains. Engine 387 was released from Parsons Shop in April and is assigned to the Texas Special and Blue Bonnet. Engine 404 also has the Katy Emblem painted on the tender, which makes the second of the program to place this emblem on all Pacific Type Locomotives.

from "The M-K-T Employes" Magazine", July 1928 issue, page 196

Dunlap

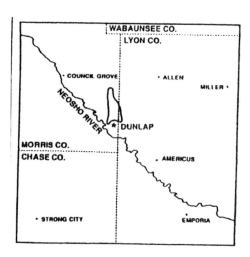

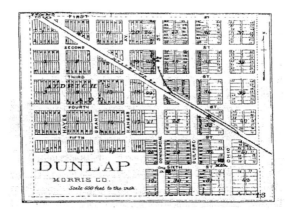

Dunlap, Kansas is located in Morris County. Before the village was incorporated, it was a busy stop on the MKT Railroad and served farmers shipping cattle, hogs and agricultural products. At first it was just a platform

MKT Depot, key point for immigrants to find new homes, jobs, and support in Dunlap

S. L. SARGENT,

REAL ESTATE,

LOAN AND COLLECTION

AGENT

DUNLAP, MORRIS COUNTY, KANSAS.

Choice Farms, both Improved and Unimproved, for Sale Cheap.

*View looking north on Commercial Street, around
1920*

*Dunlap City Hall, built of hand-hewn stone in 1914.
It burned in 1968.*

Mt. Zion Baptist Church as it stands today. Was last used in approximately 1956.

Saw mill

New cars just delivered to Dunlap, a growing and prosperous village

Livery Feed Stable

Livery and Feed Stable with three horses and rider

Dunlap Post Office

Dunlap Filling Station

Dunlap Gymnasium

The Dunlap High School

Outhouse (bathroom) by tree

Dunlap United Methodist Church

Win Bernard Hardware with his carriage out front

Dunlap Bank

Grandfather's Story

DUREAL (JEFF) HAYES - 82
Council Grove, Kansas

Artist: Tony Allard
Writer: Erleen J. Christensen

I got my nickname when we went to work for this white man and he sees me and my brother are close together and says, "I'm gonna call you Jeff and you I'm gonna call him Mutt." I went by that ever since. My brother worked for that man, rented his place for years. We'd go up there, my brother and I and he was always runnin' on with us.

That was in Alberta, near Edmonton-a little town by the name of LaDuke. I was born in Mississippi, but I don't remember it. We was small kids when we moved to Oklahoma, and we never went back. It was my older brother decided to move to Canada.

Daddy went to Colorado looking for work,and when he came back the boys had made up their mind. We took the railroad. A bunch of people moved up there- twelve cars of people, all different places. They had cheap rates for people going up there at one time, excursion rates.

My Daddy Taught His Boys to Work

Daddy and us boys in the cotton field
with the hot sun and the weeds
My brother was tired
and the row was so long

"Daddy, could I rest?"
"I'll rest you at the end of the row."

At the end of the row, Daddy cut a switch
and my brother never got tired no more

Photographer: S. Kay Stewart

Mother's Story (in her own words)

Lillian Hayes Campbell with father, Dureral Hayes

These are the stories of Lillian Campbell, who grew up in Dunlap Colony. Her Great-Grandmother came to America from Africa in the belly of a slave ship to Tennessee. She soon learned of the Underground Railroad and escaped Kentucky and came to Kansas.

I am the daughter of Duereal and Octavia Hayes. My mother, Octavia, died when I was a baby, so my grandmother, Rosetta Ragland, raised me and was a mother to me.

When I was a baby, I came down with polio and was in a very bad condition. During my illness, "Mother Ragland" rubbed me with three kinds of liniment and other things that I don't remember what she said. But with the Grace and Mercy of the Lord and her loving care, I overcame that illness and was able to live a normal life.

We lived on a farm between Council Grove, Kansas, and Dunlap, Kansas.

When it came time to start to school, my cousin, Theran Ragland, nicknamed "Bubby", and I walked about four miles or so to a little country school every day. Mom raised both of us. There are two years between our ages.

I was always afraid when it started storming with all the lightning and thundering. If it started on my way to school, I would run into any of the neighbor's

houses on the way to school without even knocking! I
would sit down in a chair until it was over with and
then I would get up and go on to school. Of course,
they would always call the school and tell the teacher
where I was. I didn't talk any more than I had to.

I had to do chores every morning before going to
school, which was milking three cows. After school, I
had my three cows to milk again, plus do other things,
such as bringing in wood and coal for our heating
stores, gathering eggs, and helping feed the pigs.

Every Saturday morning, if the weather wasn't too
bad, Mom, my cousin and I would go to the railroad
tracks and pick up coal for our heating stores and
fueling our stove. The coal was used along with wood
in order to make the wood last longer. Plus, coal gave
a real warming heat. We also used to pick up cow
chips from the field where the cows stayed at. These
cow chips burned good and put out lots of heat.

Mom planted a good garden every year with almost all
kinds of vegetables in it, so that she wouldn't have
much food to buy. She was a wonderful cook. I
learned what I know from her. She taught me to
make a little bit of something stretch and to keep the
things that were important on hand, like foods that
don't spoil, washing powder, toilet paper, towels, and
every other thing that we need and use all the time.
That way, when we didn't have any money, there
would be something to fall back on. We were poor,
but a person wouldn't know it. We were so happy.
When I left home, I was well able to take care of
myself and my family without asking people for

anything. That's why so many people thought that I really had a lot.

I was raised up not to borrow anything from anyone (and I still don't). Mom always told me, "If you don't have money to buy what you want or need, then you don't need it if you need to borrow to get it". That's why I seldom borrow anything. I tried to raise my children like that.

Farmers who would kill pigs for their meat would bring Mom the intestines and Mom would spend the whole day cleaning them without any help, moving from one shady place to another until they were finished. During that time while Mom was working so hard cleaning those messy things, I would get lost and not be seen. Every now and then, I'd look back around the corner of the house at her working. She wouldn't see me tell she was finished. She never said anything to me about not helping her, nor did she ever whip me for not helping.

But, when it came to gardening and keeping the weeds hoed out, I would get it. When I would be hoeing the weeds and a worm would get on me, I would run to the house and sit down, because I was really afraid of worms and bugs (and still am!). When Mom looked around and didn't see me, she would come to the house and give me a hit and send me back out. I would run back to the garden spot and go back to hoeing the weeds until another worm got on me, and the same thing would happen all over again. After I was grown, I would think about it off and on, how Mom should have been hard on me about not helping her with those intestines like she was about the gardening, because I was the first one in the pot eating after the chitterlings were cooked. My mom wasn't a mean woman: she just believed in doing your work and doing it well, whatever it may be.

We also had to make up our beds when we first got up in the morning, and I still do it. Mom started me out washing and ironing my own clothes when I was old enough. During the washing, I was fine, but when it came to ironing them, for some reason I had a problem. I would have more wrinkles in them than what I started with. Mom cured me of that by sprinkling them down again so I had to re-iron them again. She didn't have to do that more than twice, if that much. She made a believer out of me. I'll do my work and do it well the very first time. We didn't have any electricity for a long time. We had kerosene lamps and washing machines with handles that you had to turn with your hands. Every Saturday afternoon, we all, including Mom, would clean the house after we had been out all morning picking up coal from the railroad tracks. After everything was done, then I was allowed to play until it was time to milk my cows again and do my evening chores.

During the winter, we used to have really deep snow all the time. I really enjoyed playing in the snow and have always liked the snow.

Mom's mother lived with us too. I would dress her on the weekends. She kept Mom off of me when I had done something wrong. When I saw that Mom was going to get me, I would run to Great-Grandmother and she wouldn't let Mom hit me. It wasn't often, but whenever Mom got on me, believe me, I needed all the help I could get!

Whenever Mom had company, if we were in the room, we had to go outside to play. We weren't like the children of today. Mom didn't have to tell us, all she had to do was to look at us if we didn't move fast enough. When she had to give us that look or speak, we knew what we would get.

My dad, Duereal Hayes, would come out every weekend to visit me. It was a very long time before I knew he was my father. When we were old enough to go to Sunday school and to church, he would drive us to Dunlap. The church we went to was about ten or fifteen miles from where we lived and there were many Sundays that we walked to church.

The school we went to was one large school house with several grades and one teacher for all these different grades. I don't remember how many grades there were, but I think there weren't over four classes in each grade. I think each grade had different places to sit in the classroom and the teacher would have certain time for each grade. When I finished grade school and started high school, I made good grades and majored in sewing. I liked doing that very much and still love sewing. I stayed in trouble with my sewing teachers most of the time because I would look at the patterns half of the time and put things together without reading all the instructions.

To get to high school I had about three miles to walk to catch a ride to Dunlap. If I missed my ride, I had to walk the rest of the way. Those were my good old days, when we were walking to school about 3 country miles. I had to wear those long, brown socks and long underwear in the winter time. You know how some children can be when they are not in the low class, making fun of you because you are wearing those kinds of clothes, so when I would get to the railroad underpass, I would pull my long underwear off and hide them under a rock and roll my long socks down and go on to school. When school was out, on my way home, when we got to the train track underpass, I would put my underwear back on. You can imagine how cold they were. That went on for a few years until one day, when it came time to put them on again, I couldn't find them! I had forgotten which rock I put them under. That ended wearing long underwear for me.

One time Bubby and I were playing outside. I was on the other side of the house when he threw a rock over the house and hit me in the head and knocked me out for a while. I had a knot on my head for a long time. Another day, we were supposed to be helping Mom hoe the weeds. We got to playing for a while and Theron did something to me, so I started running after him. He got a head start on me and stretched out a wire that was around a pole. I was running so hard that I didn't see the wire and ran into it. I hit it so hard that it threw me so high in the air that I heard the angels before I hit the ground. If we weren't doing something together, he was always doing something to me.

One day, Theron decided to build an airplane, so he built one out of wood. He pulled it up on a shed roof, got in it and pushed it off thinking that it was going to fly. It didn't. It fell on the ground with him in it and hit the ground so hard that it scared him so bad that he couldn't move or talk for a long time. It even scared me! He didn't build anything else after that.

Mom was very loving and understanding. She taught me and cousin Theron what to do to take care of ourselves without depending on others. Theron could cook as good as I could when he wanted to.

Mother would sell eggs and milk. A man would come out from town and pick them up every week. When mom would go to town during the daytime, our neighbor girl and I would steal two or three eggs and make ourselves an egg omelet, not thinking that Mother would miss them. Then I was in trouble for that, so we didn't do that too often.

When I became a teenager, I spent most of my time out on another farm which was my Uncle Reuben Hayes' (my father's brother). These two brothers were married to two sisters. My father, Duereal, was married to Octavia Ragland and my uncle Reuben was married to her sister, Lucia (?) Ragland. So we children were really first cousins. The older ones, Bill, George and Violet and I used to go out and around to different places with friends. We would go to Lawrence, Emporia and Lyon, where there were other teenagers that we ran around with. So if we were good and did our chores right and like we were supposed to without being told, we would get to go out for the weekend. That's when we would choose one of the places to go. But if we did anything wrong to make Uncle Reuben upset with us, well, we didn't go anywhere. I looked upon Uncle Reuben as my second Dad.

I ended up getting married very young. I didn't know anything about the outside world. I had babies back to back. My step-mother, Callie, was very good to me. She would come over to my house and talk to me, telling me about different things of life, like what and how to do the right things. She also helped and showed me lots of things about sewing, but I learned to crochet on my own. She was a very understanding woman, even when I had been doing things that were not right. She would talk to me about it and tell me that what I was doing weren't right. She didn't tell my dad everything that I was doing or trying to do, especially when I was trying to run wild before I got married. She also talked to me after I got married about things that I should know and didn't know. She was a very sweet and loving step-mother. She would take care of my babies when I had another in the hospital. She was very good to all of my children and helped me a lot with them.

I would take my children to go out to the farm to visit my mom. They got along with her okay. For some reason, my oldest daughter told me after she became grown that she was afraid of Mom. My sons, Duereal and Virgil went and spent part of a summer with her. At that time they were almost teenagers. Duereal made a little motor car that summer. They would go into town to Council Grove off and on while staying out on the farm with Mom. At the time, Mom was married to a man named Givins. He was an okay man.

I didn't know my birth-mother, but Mom Ragland told me that she was a good mechanic. She could take any car apart and fix it by replacing parts and putting it back together again. Other than that, I don't really know too much about my parents. What little I know about my Dad is what he told me. He was born in Mississippi and moved to Canada with his folks when he was very young. He was about eight at the time. His mother was a white woman and his dad was black. His family was quite large. He lived in Canada until he was a full grown man. My mother got in touch with him by writing to him from a newspaper ad. At first it was my mother's sister that started writing to him. They wrote back and forth for a while. Finally, he started to Kansas by working his way from town to town. When he would run out of money, he would stay in a town working for whoever he could to get enough money to go further. When his money would run out again, he'd work some more to earn more money to continue the journey. He did his traveling by catching trains by jumping in the grain cars, not letting anyone see him. After he got to Kansas, he and my mother's sister got together and started going steady together and finally got married. They had a little girl and moved back to Canada for a while. Something happened that his wife got sick and died, but not before they lost their baby first. After several years, he came back to Kansas and married my mother.

Lillian Hayes Campbell--In 2008 she was entered into the bowling hall of fame in Salina, Kansas.

Dunlap Elementary School

Great Grandmother's Dream (In her own words)

I had a dream—not just any old kind of dream, but a dream that only God could do. Guess what? I, Betty Gupton, was a slave. We came from Western Africa in the belly of a ship.

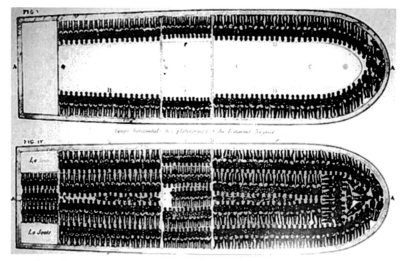

On the voyage to America, slaves were packed into ships

The children were thrown in the middle like chicken in a pin.

I never really knew what true darkness or hunger or thirst felt like. In Africa, we picked berries and the men hunted every day and the women cooked, so we ate whenever we were hungry.

When the ship landed, we were bathed in water and oil was put on us. We were taken to a big farm called a plantation. There we were not able to pick berries or eat when we were hungry. We worked from sunup to sundown.

 **TO BE SOLD** on board the
Ship *Bance-Ifland*, on tuefday the 6th
of *May* next, at *Afhley-Ferry*, a choice
cargo of about 250 fine healthy

NEGROES,

juft arrived from the
Windward & Rice Coaft.
—The utmoft care has
already been taken, and
fhall be continued, to keep them free from
the leaft danger of being infected with the
SMALL-POX, no boat having been on
board, and all other communication with
people from *Charles-Town* prevented.

Auftin, Laurens, & Appleby.

N. B. Full one Half of the above Negroes have had the
SMALL-POX in their own Country.

*Newspaper advertisement for a slave sale in South Carolina in
the late 1700s*

The only thing that did not change for us was being able to look at the clouds. Sometimes we could see a cat or a boat, but every time she would see the figure of an adult and a child, but it was not clear if it was a woman or a man. Looking at the clouds was the only time we really felt free. Freedom was something we all thought about; it was something we all had in Western Africa where we could go and do as we needed to do, in peace.

Looking at the clouds

On Sunday in a thing called church, we had a preacher that explained what was being said because he was able to read the Bible. My mother and I worked in the Big House, so luckily I was able to learn to read while I watched the children. I thought they would not sell me and the other women that worked in the Big House.

Next morning we found out that she and her mother were going to be sold. Where was God? The preacher said that God would never leave us. (Hebrew 13:5)

Every night I would have this same dream, but new things would appear. At the bottom of the road would be railroad tracks, but they were on top of the ground and people were getting off a boxcar and running up the hill to the house and I could actually see my children and they were free.

Sculpture that stands in Oberlin, Ohio, to honor everyone who was involved in the Underground Railroad (UGRR)

We made our way to freedom through the Underground Railroad and went to Kansas. To keep from being caught we never traveled in a straight line. So we went first to White City and then went back to Dunlap.

The White City Rock Island Depot, 1924.   *The Prairie Post, Joann Kahnt, Editor*

White City Depot

Neosho River and old post office--The Neosho River ran though Council Grove and there was an Underground Railroad tunnel to the old post office. At night slaves would go to White City then to Dunlap, Kansas, the second largest Black settlement in Kansas where the first Literary and Business Academy was.

Tunnel from the river to the old Post Office

Madonna of the Trail statue in Council Grove, KS—one of twelve Madonna of the Trail statues in the U.S.

She also told of slaves getting out the green railroad box car on the train and running up the driveway. She would feed them, and send them on their way with some food. I, Karen, was there when a dove came and told her that Mrs. Johnson was sick. I put the two children in the wagon and Grandmother

(Tinney) held down the fence to let us get though. Mrs. Johnson was sick. I decided to take the road back to the house. That route was so long that it was dark when I got back.

Grandmother worked at the Moxley's farm doing domestic work. She also sold eggs and milk. Also, she said if she ever went to city she would die because the air was too dirty.

She showed me how to plant sweet potatoes in hills and how to cut weeds in the heat of the day. One very important thing I learned from Grandmother was to just look at what needs to be done today. Grandmother had a huge field that had to be hand-weeded. I would look at the whole field and be overwhelmed by all that had to be done, but she only looked at the plot she wanted to do that day. And she got it all done, and before I knew it, the field was cut!

Memorial Monument

to

Henry L. Davis

And

Early Ex-Slave Settlers

to

Dunlap, Kansas

Jack Davis son of a mixed-race couple, didn't grow up with his Mother." I was the only my dad had. He never married, and I haven't either. Because of racial differences, families would not let them marry". As a child, he called his aunt Velera Davis "Mommie," and would listen to her stories. One of my favorite memories of growing up in Kansas was a sense of connectedness. The older people were always 'Cousin' of 'Aunt.' It seemed like big, extended family.

(A Monument to Exodusters by Robin Van Arken, Aug. 23, 2011-C.G Republican Newspaper)

My grandfather, Henry L. Davis, according to my Mommy(Aunt Velara Davis), was born a slave. His mother escaped and carried her baby to Kansas when the owner threatened to sell him. Her man left her in Tonganoxie, Ks. She later moved to Soden's Grove outside Emporia by the mill. There Sam Robinson courted and married her. They moved to his farm on Wright Creek where Henry grew up.

Great-Grandma Davis-Robinson and Sam Robinson saw that Henry and his brother Sam got an education.

Henry met and married Ida May Maddox and started a family. He worked and got several teams. With them, he worked on the railroad and other jobs. He was on the Americus School Board at one time. In 1904 he and Ida purchased this land from the original "Homesteader". He then purchased a house and drug it 6 miles across the prairie with his teams.

Here he became a very prosperous farmer. He had little money, but he had FOOD !! All the older people I talked to when I was a child, told me they could come to the "Davis" place and EAT !!

When the years creeped up on him, my Uncle Roy (the eldest son) did not want to take over the farm (He had his own place), so the second son, my father, Ralph H. Davis, took over the family farm. When I came along, my Daddy bought everyone out.

My GrandPa and my Daddy built up quite a farm. They raised livestock - hogs, cattle, poultry, and horses , and crops. The family also had ½ acre garden plus garden crops in the fields.
,

My Dad died in 1969. The family tried to sell everything. I managed to keep the land. I had a hard time trying to get equipment and livestock. My Mom and her son took over (or at least they tried to) There was several attempts to sell part or all of the farm, BUT, the agreement was to keep the farm in the family. When it was all over, I was the last Davis left,,,,, BUT the place was completely destroyed !!!!!!

At the end of March, 2010 ,, the Doctors at the "V A Medical Center" in Albuquerque, New Mexico said I had Pancreatic cancer,, Stage 4,, terminal ! You have 3 months to live.

So,, I sold the farm with the provision I could build a memorial. With treatment at the "Raymond G. Murphy VA Medical Center" in Albuquerque, New Mexico and God's help, I have survived to build a memorial.

This is what I built.

Putting the sign on   It's up!

The Sign reads:

From the mid 1800's to the 1890's, many ex-slaves moved from the South and settled near te Neosho River near Dunlap, Ks. They made their homes in Lyon, Morris, Chase counties where they raised their families in FREEDOM! The "Crash of "29" and the dirty 30's was too much for most. They moved to the large Cities. Some sent goods and funds back. Henry L. Davis was born a slave. His Mother escaped and carried her baby to Kansas and FREEDOM! As a young man he worked on the railroad with his team of mules and purchased this property

From the homesteader. He was a well-respected man. He raised his family here and he died here. His second son-Ralph H. Davis- took over the family farm. He was very successful and respected farmer. Ralph's son tried, but serious vandalism in the 1980's destroyed everything. The Harness farm was sold in the 1990's. All other farms owned by descendent of an ex-slave.

(End of sign) On a 14x24 piece welded below with 2.6" SS pipe holding it: So Goes History

(Signed) by Jackie L. Davis

Jack and Jim Sharp at the first Verwing of the Finished Monament

My Thanks to :

Clayton and Pat Finney of Americus, Ks
    For their permission and support of this

Frank Cappleman of Rocky Mountain Tank Aztec, NM
    He Donated Stainless Steel plate

Richard Trujillo of U S AirWeld Farmington NM
    He donated welding Supplies

Terry Lyon of Allen/Americus
His Dad told him to call me "Uncle Jack"
    His labor , Machinery , tools , and place made this happen

Bob and Connie Palmer
    for their support , photography , and enduring friendship

Ustaine Talley   Lifelong friend and almost Step-Sister
    For her encouragement, article, historical knowledge and
    contacts

Penni Malott Niece/Daughter of my heart
    She tried to be Uncle Jack's nurse, helper, and housecleaner
    when Dr said I was dying of cancer

        Thanks   Jackie L Davis

Appendix: Glossary

The Underground Railroad from the 1800s often used terms similar to those used by railroaders: agent, conductors, track, etc. This led to confusion, especially after locomotive and railcars which were utilized during escapes.

Abolitionist: A person who advocated for the end of slavery, ranging from a gradual process (a gradualist) to the radical who wanted an immediate end with equal rights for blacks (an immediate emancipationist).

Agent: Someone who provided assistance to freedom seekers. This person may or may not have been an opponent of slavery. An agent may have provided food, clothing, transportation or shelter.

Colonization: A movement to take people out of slavery in America to freedom in Africa.

Conductor: Someone who led freedom seekers from place to place. Early Underground Railroad terms related to jobs on railroads.

Free black: A person of African descent who was not enslaved. Some free blacks were never enslaved; others were manumitted (provided legal freedom from slavery.)

Freedom seekers: A person who escaped the institution of slavery. This flight was not always north and was usually unaided until reaching a Northern state. *Escape, run-away, and fugitive* were terms used in the 1880s.

Fugitive: Describe someone who escaped from slavery. This negative term was used to imply that this person broke the law, even in Free states where slaveholding was forbidden.

Maroon colony: This is an isolated community settled by freedom seekers.

Master: The male (Mistress for female) owner, recognized by law, of a person he1ood in slavery during the antebellum period.

Self-emancipated: This is not legally freed from enslavement by an owner or the legal system, but by one's own determination.

Slave hunter: They were also known as a slave catcher or bounty hunter, this person sought freedom seekers for reward money. Free Blacks were sometimes kidnapped and sold.

Slave Patroller: A person who rode in Southern areas looking for any black person without a pass (a written note of permission to travel without supervision.

Stock: Belief or faith in the abolitionist cause. Stockholders donated food, money, of clothing.

Underground Railroad: Is the means by which those escaping, and those helping them, effected their flight. Though the term was coined in the 1830s, today it encompasses all manner of flight from an earlier time until slavery ended. Many of the enslaved escaped without help.

Appendix: Underground Railroad Chronology

Colonies and areas of cities in Kansas where "Exodusters"

settled in 1879-1881

I singleton's Colony-Cherokee   1873-
"Negro Hill"

II Nicodemus Colony – Graham –   1877-
"demus"

III Hodgeman Centre= Hodgemen-   1877

IV Morton City- Hodgemen   1878

V Dunlap   - Morris   1878

VI Kansas City   Wyandotte   1879-1880
"Mississippi town or

"Juniper Bottoms"
Rattlebone Hollow"

VII Parsons Labette   1879
"Scuffletown"or
"Mudtown"

VIII Wabaunsee Colony-Wabaunsee 1879

LX Topeka   -Shawnee   1880
     "Tennesseetown or

     "Redmonville"

"Mudtown"

Underground Railroad Chronology

1607   Jamestown, Virginia, settled by English colonists.

1619   **Twenty Africans are shipped to Jamestown, Virginia, on Dutch ships.**

1642   Virginia Colony enacts laws to fine those who harbor or assist runaway slaves.

1660   **Virginia Colony legalizes slavery.**

1741   North Carolina colony enacts law to prosecute any person caught assisting runaways.

1775   **The Pennsylvania Abolition Society is established to protect fugitives and freed blacks unlawfully held in bondage.**

1776   North American colonies declare independence from Great Britain.

1777-1804 Northern states abolish slavery through state constitutions.

1787   The Northwest Ordinance prevents slavery from existing in the new federal territories.
The Free African Society of Philadelphia, an abolitionist

group, is organized by Richard Allen and Absalom Jones.

1793 Fugitive Slave Act becomes a federal law, allowing slave-owners, their agents, or attorneys to seize fugitive slaves in free states and territories.

1794 Mother Bethel African Methodist Episcopal Church is established in Philadelphia, PA

1800 Nat Turner and John Brown are born. Gabriel Prosser stages an unsuccessful slave insurrection in Henrico County, VA

1804 The Underground Railroad is "incorporated" after slave owner, Gen. Thomas Boudes of Columbia, PA refuses to surrender escaped slave to authorities.

1816 The Seminole Wars begin in Florida as a result of many slaves taking refuge with Seminole Indians.

1818 As a response to the Fugitive Slave Act (1793), abolitionists use the "underground" to assist slaves to escape into Ohio and Canada.

1820 The Missouri Compromise admits Missouri and Maine as slave and free states, respectively. The measure establishes the 36/30 parallel of latitude as a dividing line between free and slave areas of the territories.

1821 Kentucky representatives present resolution to Congress protesting Canada's reception of fugitives slaves.

1822 Former slave Denmark Vesey leads a slave uprising in Charleston, SC

1829   Black abolitionist David Walker issues **David Walker's Appeal**. Afterwards, several slave revolts occurred throughout the South.

1830   **Levi Coffin leaves North Carolina, settles in Indiana and continues abolitionist activities.**

1831   William Lloyd Garrison prints first issues of his anti-slavery newspaper, **The Liberator.** Black entrepreneur and abolitionist Robert Forten becomes chief financial supporter of the publication.
Nat Turner stages insurrection in Southampton County, VA

1832   **Louisiana presents resolution requesting Federal Government to arrange with Mexico to permit runaway slaves from Louisiana to be reclaimed when found on foreign soil.**

1834   National Antislavery Society organizes Underground Railroad as a response to pro-slavery argument.

1838   **Underground Railroad is "formally organized."**
Black abolitionist Robert Purvis becomes chairman of the General Vigilance Committee and "president" of the Underground Railroad.

1842   Supreme Court rules in **Prigg v. Pennsylvania** that state officials are not required to assist in the return of fugitives slaves.

1847   **Frederick Douglass edits an anti-slavery newspaper, the "North Star."**

1849   Harriet Tubman makes her escape from Maryland.

1850	The Compromise of 1850 attempts to settle the slavery issue. As part of the Compromise, a new Fugitive Slave Act is added to enforce the 1793 law and allow slaveholders to retrieve slaves in northern states and free territories.
1852	Harriet Beecher Stowe's Uncle Tom's Cabin is published as a response to the pro-slavery argument.
1857	Supreme Court declares in Scott v. Sandford that blacks are not U.S. citizens, and slaveholders have the right to take slaves in free areas of the country.
1859	John Brown's failed raid on a federal arsenal and armory in Harper's Ferry, VA, which was aimed at starting a general slave insurrection.
1860	Republican candidate Abraham Lincoln is elected President of the United States.
1861	The Civil War begins.
1863	President Lincoln issues the Emancipation Proclamation which declares "all persons held as slaves within any state ... be in rebellion against the United States shall be then ... forever free."
1865	Civil War ends.
	Thirteenth Amendment is amended to the U.S. Constitution abolishing slavery permanently.

This Chronology provided by the National Park Service.

Appendix: Posters of going to Kansas

CASH!

All persons that have SLAVES to dispose of, will do well by giving me a call, as I will give the **HIGHEST PRICE FOR Men, Women, & CHILDREN.**

Any person that wishes to sell, will call at Hill's tavern, or at Shannon Hill for me, and any information they want will be promptly attended to.

Thomas Griggs.

Charlestown, May 7, 1835.

PRINTED AT THE FREE PRESS OFFICE, CHARLESTOWN.

HO !

—FOR—

Dunlap Colony.

Morris County, Kansas.

The Most Prosperous Colony in the State.

75,000 Acres

Of Government Land yet remains to be settled.

THE Kansas Freedman's Relief Association has discontinued its work as a chartered organization. None need expect help or direction from such source any longer. The tide of immigration of colored people, however, still continues. I cannot stand idly by when I see so much need of intelligent direction to my people. It is a great mistake for the leaders of bodies of our people from the South who wish to settle on

Encouraging black settlers to make Dunlap their home, this column touts the attributes of the colony, including an "Industrial School" established by "Rev. Mr. Snodgrass."

GO TO KANSAS,

On September 5th, 1877,

Can do so for $5.00

IMMIGRATION.

Whereas, We, the colored people of Lexington, Ky., knowing that there is an abundance of choice lands now belonging to the Government, have assembled ourselves together for the purpose of locating on said lands. Therefore,

Be it Resolved, That we do now organize ourselves into a Colony, as follows:— Any person wishing to become a member of this Colony can do so by paying the sum of one dollar ($1.00), and this money is to be paid by the first of September, 1877, in installments of twenty-five cents at a time, or otherwise as may be desired.

Resolved, That this Colony has agreed to consolidate itself with the Nicodemus Town, Solomon Valley, Graham County, Kansas, and can only do so by entering the vacant lands now in their midst, which costs $5.00.

Resolved, That this Colony shall consist of seven officers—President, Vice-President, Secretary, Treasurer, and three Trustees. President—M. M. Bell; Vice-President —Isaac Talbott; Secretary—W. J. Niles; Treasurer—Daniel Clarke; Trustees—Jerry Lee, William Janes, and Abner Webster.

Resolved, That this Colony shall have from one to two hundred militia, more or less, as the case may require, to keep peace and order, and any member failing to pay in his dues, as aforesaid, or failing to comply with the above rules in any particular, will not be recognized or protected by the Colony.

Last Chance Store where Chris. & Jennie were hidden in the basement before being taken to the Kaw Indian Reservation until after the Civil War.

Go to Kansas,
On September 5, 1877
Can do so for $5.00

Immigration

Whereas, We, the colored people of Lexington, KY., knowing that there is an abundance of choice lands now belonging to the Government, have assembled ourselves together for the locating on said land. Therefore,

Be it Resolved, that we do now organize ourselves into a Colony, as follows: Any person wishing to become a member of this colony can do so by paying the sum of one dollar ($1), and this money is to be paid by the first of September, 1877, in installments of twenty-five cents at a time, or otherwise as may be desired.

Resolved, that this Colony has agreed to consolidate itself with the Nicodemus Towns, Solomon Valley, Graham County, Kansas, and can only do so by entering the vacant lands in their midst, which costs $5.oo.

Resolved, that this Colony shall consist of seven officers- President, Vice-President, Secretary, Treasurer, and three Trustees. President- M.M. Bell; Vice-President-Isaac Talbott; Secretary –W.J. Niles; Treasurer- Daniel Clarke; Trustees- Jerry Lee, William Jones, and Abner Webster.

Resolved, that this Colony shall have from one to two hundred militia, more or less as the case may require, to keep peace and order, and any member failing to pay in dues, as aforesaid, or failing to comply with the above rules in any particular, will not be recognized or protected by the Colony.

"Last chance where Chas & Jenner were hidden in the basement before being taken to the Kaw Indian Reservation until after the Civil War."

> ### TRAIL RUTS
>
> The swales before you are 20 feet wide. They were made from the thousands of

HO! FOR SUNNY KANSAS!

FRIENDS AND FELLOW CITIZENS:

I have just returned from the Singleton Settlement, in Morris County, Kansas, where I left my people is one of the finest countries for a poor man in the World. I am prepared to answer any and all questions that may be asked. The Singleton Settlement is near Dunlap, Morris County, a new town just started on the Missouri, Kansas & Texas Railway. The surrounding country is fine rolling prairie. Plenty of stone and water, and wood on the streams. Plenty of coal within twenty-five miles.

I have this to say to all:

Now is the Time to Go to Kansas.

Land is cheap, and it is being taken up very fast. There is plenty for all at present.

BENJAMIN SINGLETON,
President.

ALFRED D. DeFRANTE, Secretary,
JOSEPH KEEDLE, Agent, Real Estate and Homestead Association.

For full information, address COLUMBUS M. JOHNSON, Topeka, Kansas.

General Agent.

HO

FOR SUNNY KANSAS

FRIENDS AND FELLOW CITIZENS:

I have just returned from Singleton Settlement, in Morris County, Kansas, where I left my people in one of the finest countries for a poor man in the world. I am prepared to answer any and all questions that may be asked. The Singleton Settlement is near Dunlap, Morris County, a new town just started on the Missouri, Kansas, & Texas Railway. The surrounding county is fine rolling prairie. Plenty of stone and water, and wood on the streams. Plenty of coal within twenty –five miles. I have this to say to all:

NOW IS THE TIME TO GO TO KANSAS *Land is cheap, and it is being taken up fast. There is plenty for all at present.*

Benjamin Singleton,
President

Appendix: What If There Were No Blacks

This is a story of a little boy named Theo, who woke up one morning and asked Mom "What if there were no black people in the world?" Well, Mom thought about that for a moment and then said "Son, follow me around today and let's just see what it would be like if there were no black people in the world. Get dressed and we will get started.

Theo ran to his room to put on his clothes and shoes. But there were no shoes, and his clothes were all wrinkled. He looked for the iron, but when reached for the ironing board, it was no longer there. You see Sarah Boone, a Black woman, inverted the ironing board and Jan E. Matzelinger, a Black man invented the shoe lasting machine.

"Oh well, Mom said, "Go and do your hair." Theo ran in his room to comb his hair, but the comb was not there. You see, Walter Sammons, a Black man, invented the comb. Theo decided to just brush was gone. You see Lydia O. Newman, a Black female invented the brush.

Well, he was a sight, no shoes, wrinkled clothes, hair a mess without inventions of Madam C. J. Walker, well, you get the picture. Mom told Theo, "Let's do the chores around the house and then take a trip to the grocery store."

Theo's job was to sweep the floor. He swept and swept and swept.

When he reached for the dustpan. It was not having any luck. "Well, son. " Mom said. "We should wash the clothes and prepare a list for the grocery store.

When he was finished. Theo went to place the clothes, but it was not there. You see Lloyd P. Ray, a Black man, invented the dustpan. So he swept his pile of dirt over in the corner and left it there. He then decided to mop the floor, but the mop was gone. You see, Thomas W. Stewart, a Black man, invented the mop.

Theo thought to himself, "I'm not having any luck. " "Well, son," Mom said. "We should wash the clothes and prepare a list for the grocery store. When he was finished, Theo Went to place the clothes in the dryer. You see George T. Samon, a Black man, invent the clothes dryer. Theo got a pencil and some paper to prepare the list for the market , but the lead was broken as well, he was out of luck because , John Love, a Black man, invented the pencil sharpener. He reached for the pen, but it was not there because William Purvis, a Black man invented the foundation pen. As a matter of fact, Lee Burridge invented the type writing machine and W.A Lavette, the printing press.

So they decided to head out to the market. Well, when Theo opened the door, he noticed the grass was as high as he was tall. You see the lawnmower was invented by John Burr, a Black man.

They made their way over to the car and found that it just wouldn't go. You see Robert Spikes, a Black man, invented the automatic gear shift and Joseph

Gammel invented the supercharge system for internal combustion engines.

They noticed that the few car that were moving were running into each other and having wreck because there was no traffic signals. A black man, Garrett A. Morgan invented the traffic light.

Well, was getting late, so they walked to the market, got their groceries and returned home. Just when they were about to put away the milk, eggs and butter, they noticed the refrigerator was gone. You see John Standard, a Black man, invented the refrigerator. So they put food on the counter.

By this time, they noticed it was getting mighty cold Theo went to turn up the heat and what do you know, it was not there. You see, Alive Parker, a Black female, invented the heating furnace. Even in the summer time they would have been out luck, because Frederick Jones, a Black man invented the air conditioner.

It was almost time for Theo's father to arrive home. He usually took the bus, but there was no bus because its precursor was the electric trolley, invented by another Black man, Elbert T. Robinson. He usually took the elevator from his office on the 20th floor, but there was no elevator because Alexander Miles, a Black man, invented the elevator. He usually dropped office mail at a nearby mail box, but it no longer was there because Phillip Downing, a Black man, invented the mailbox and William Barry invented the postmarking and canceling machine.

Theo sat at the kitchen table with his head in his hands. When his father arrived he asked "Why are you sitting in the dark? Why?? Because Lewis Howard Latimer, a Black man, invented the filament within the light bulb.

Theo quickly learned what it would be like if there were not black people in the world.
Not to mention if he were ever sick and needed blood, which led to his starting the world's first blood bank.
And what if a family member had to have heart surgery. This would not been possible without Dr. Daniel Hale Williams, a Black doctor, who performed first open heart surgery.
So if you ever wonder, like Theo, where we would be without Blacks? Well, it's pretty plain to see, we could very well still be in the dark!!!

Barbara Leany 1998

Cookbook Index

Tips

Beverages

Eggs

Grains and Cereals

Vegetables

Potatoes

Sauces

Meats

Leftovers Meats

Fish

Soup

Poultry

Cheese

Salads

Quick Breads

Cakes

Cookies

Odds and Ends

Cooking back in the time on a Range

An Average range weighed 400-600 pounds
Can you believe that women moved these
any times with little help from the men folk?
Recipes were in the heads of many people and past down
from generation to generation. It was only by trial and
error to get the recipe just the way the cook wanted it.
(Only the literate used written recipes)
Some of the tips used
when shopping and using a range:
One had to know all the measurements of the range
before purchase, otherwise the range might not fit
through the door or the ceiling may be too low.
Many times the homes were made around the
measurements of the range.
Larger flues produce more heat.
Does it have space to heat was tubs behind?
Determine the size of front draft,
no one wants smoke in the house.

What will you use to burn in the range,
cow chips, wood, coal?
Caution had to be used as to know how to fire a
wood range and keep an even temperature for baking.

It was very easy to burn oneself on a range.
Butter was often times rubbed over the place that was
Burnt to prevent further damage, so they thought.
Another tip was to put vanilla on a burn
To take the sting out.

Cow Chips could produce an awful odor that
Sometimes permeated the food.
To keep flute from rusting use soft cloth saturated
in cooking oil, rub pipe and top of range well,
remove excess.
If excess is not removed smoking may occur.

When using coal oil to start range
Use dried corn cobs or sticks
Of wood dipped into the can
And carefully toss in.
This is much better than pouring
Coal oil over coal or wood,
As fire starts rapidly after applying oil.

Helpful Tips

A spoonful of dry material is measured by filling the spoon, then leveling with a knife.

A half of spoonful is measured by cutting in half Lengthwise; a fourth spoonful by cutting crosswise a little nearer the handle of the spoon.

A cupful of liquid is measured by setting the cup on a level surface, and filling it as full as it will hold. (Every cup was different in them days!!!)

To measure fats, pack solidly into cup or spoon And even off with a knife.

When dry, liquid and fat ingredients are used in Same recipe, measure in order, always using same cup.

Salt spoons and pepper spoons were used when Measuring salt and pepper. Even if a recipe said one teaspoon or tablespoon, the salt and pepper spoons were adjusted to fit the recipe.

Combining:

Next to measuring, comes care in combining-a fact not always recognized by the inexperienced.

Three ways are considered:

Stirring

To stir, mix by using a circular motion (always in the same direction), widening the circles until all is blended.

Beating

To beat, turn the ingredients over and over continually, bringing the under part to the surface, and entangling air, and allowing the spoon to be constantly brought in contact with the bottom of the dish throughout the process.

Cutting and Folding

To cut and fold, introduce one mixture into another. This can be accomplished by two motions of the spoon, a repeated vertical downward motion known as cutting, and turning over and over of a mixture each time the spoon comes in contact with the bottom of the bowl; these repeated motions are used until a thorough blending is desired.

By stirring ingredients are mixed; by beating a large amount of air is enclosed; by cutting and folding, two mixtures are blended, and the air already introduced by a former motion is prevented from escaping.

Beverages

Beverage Tips:

Tea and coffee pots require a lot of care, if supreme results are to be obtained. Keep them perfectly clean. First take sand and rub on the inside to remove all grounds. Next wash with clean rain water, then rinse with boiling rain water continue until pot is clean. When clean leave uncovered until completely dry. Never reuse boiled water when making tea or coffee.

Put a clean white pot holder in the bottom of the teakettle. It takes up the alkali, through keeping your kettle clean on the inside.
Change to clean potholder every wash day.

Boiled Coffee

1 cup coffee grounds	1 cup cold water
1 egg	6 cups boiling water

Scald a granite ware coffee pot. Wash egg, break and beat slightly. Dilute with one-half of the cold water, add crushed egg shell and mix with coffee. Turn into coffee pot, pour on boiling water, and stir thoroughly. Place on front of range and boil three minutes. If not boiled, coffee is cloudy, if boiled too long, too much tannic acid is developed. The spout of the pot should be covered or stuffed with soft paper to prevent escape of fragrant aroma. Stir and pour some in a cup to be sure spout is free from grounds. Return to coffee pot and repeat. Add remaining cold water, which perfects clearing. Cold water being heavier than hot water, sinks to the bottom, carrying the ground with it. Place back on the range for ten minutes, where coffee will not be boiled, but kept warm.

Serve at once for delicious coffee.

Filtered Coffee

1 cup finely ground coffee
6 cups boiling water

Place coffee in strainer, strainer in coffee pot, and pot on the range. Add gradually boiling water and allow it to filter. Cover between additions of water. If desired stronger, re-filter.

For best result pour and serve at once.

Cocoa

3 tablespoons cocoa
A few grains of salt
1'4 cup sugar

4 cups fresh cow's milk
¾ cup boiling water

Scald cow's milk. Mix cocoa, sugar and salt, add remaining water and boil one minute; pour into scalded milk. Beat two minutes, using egg beater, when froth will form preventing scum which is so unsightly, this is known as milling.

Cocoa can be made in advance and reheated in a double boiler to use when needed. Brown sugar may be substituted for white sugar. For an interesting cocoa add a couple drops of your favorite flavoring.

Chocolate

1 ½ squares unsweetened chocolate	1 cup boiling water
	4 tablespoons sugar
	3 cups cow's milk.
Few grains salt	

Scald cow's milk. Melt the chocolate in small granite sauce pan placed over boiling water, add sugar, salt and gradually boiling water; when smooth, place on range and boil one minute; add to scalded milk and serve in chocolate cups with fresh whipped cream. One and one-half ounces vanilla chocolate may be substituted for unsweetened chocolate, being sweetened, less sugar is required.

Tea

Tea should never be boiled nor steeped for any length of time, as the tannic acid will be extracted. Fresh boiled water should always be used to pour onto tea.

Scald an earthen or china pot, put in two teaspoonfuls of tea and pour over them one pint of fresh boiling water, let stand five minutes in a warm place. Serve immediately.

Lemon and or oranges and apples may be served in tea. Wipe fruit carefully. Cut into thin slices and remove seeds. If slices are large, cut in sections, a whole clove may be stuck in each section.

Garnish with mint and cinnamon sticks if desired.

Eggs

Looking back in time at what Kansan's believed about eggs:

Eggs are the best type of protein foods. The white of the egg is composed of albumin, water and mineral matter, the yolk contains in addition to these, fat in the form of oil; the mineral matter in the yolk is very valuable.

Eggs contain no starch, so should be eaten with bread, rice or potatoes. Owing to their highly concentrated state, they should not be eaten alone; the stomach requires bulk, in order to digestion may be carried out properly.

Egg albumin coagulates at a temperature of 160 degrees Fahrenheit, becoming white and firm, but tender, soft, and jelly-like; at 200 degrees Fahrenheit it becomes hard, close grained and somewhat tough; at 212 degrees Fahrenheit it is a firm, compact solid; eggs should thus be cooked at 160 degrees Fahrenheit for perfection.

When taken eggs to market make sure to wash them carefully then put them in a cool dark place. Promote that the shells can be used for cleaning coffee pots and aiding in laundry soaps.

Another look at cooking protein, such as eggs. When cooking protein foods such as eggs or fish remember not to really boil them but simmer them in cooked water just below the boiling point. Greater tenderness results from cooking longer at lower temperature since boiling toughens protein.

Soft Cooked Eggs

Have ready a granite saucepan containing broiling water. Carefully put in with spoon the number of eggs desired, covering them with water. Remove saucepan to back of range where water will not boil. Cook from six to eight minutes if liked "soft boiled"; forty to forty-five minutes if liked "hard boiled". Eggs may be cooked by placing in cold water and allowing water to heat gradually until the boiling point is reached, when they will be "soft boiled". In using hard boiled eggs for making other dishes, when taken from the hot water they should be plunged into cold water to prevent, if possible, discoloration of yolks.

If an egg cracks during the boiling process add vinegar to the water. This seals the egg and the cooking time can be continued.

Poached Eggs

Have a shallow pan nearly full of boiling salted water, remove scum and reduce temperature until water is motionless, break an egg into a saucer and slip into the water; when a film has formed over the yolk and the with Is firm, take up with a simmer and place on toast, which has been trimmed into shape. Tip: cover pan when poaching the egg and they will not stick.

Scrambled Eggs

5 Eggs
½ cup milk
½ teaspoon salt

¼ tsp. black pepper
2 tablespoons butter

Beat eggs with silver fork, add salt, pepper and milk. Heat omelet pan, put in butter and when melted turn in mixture. Cook until creamy consistency is obtained, stirring and scraping from bottom of the pan.

Plain Omelet

4eggs
4 tablespoons milk (goat milk is wonderful)

½ teaspoon salt
2 tablespoons butter

Beat eggs slightly, just enough to blend the yolks and whites, add the milk and seasonings. Put butter in hot pan; when melted turn in the mixture; as it cooks prick and pick up with a fork until the whole is of creamy consistency. Place on hotter part of range that it may brown quickly underneath. Fold and turn on hot platter.

French Omelet

4 eggs	1 tablespoon butter
½ teaspoon salt	1 ½ cups thin white
Few grains pepper	sauce
4 tablespoons hot water	

Separate yolks from whites. Beat yolk until thick and lemon colored, add salt, pepper, and hot water. Beat whites until stiff and dry, cutting and folding them into the first mixture until they have taken up mixture. Heat pan and well butter sides and bottom. Turn in mixture, spread evenly, place on range where it will cook slowly, occasionally turning the pan so that the omelet will brown evenly. When well "puffed" and delicately brown underneath, place pan on center grate of oven to finish cooking the top. The omelet is cooked it if is firm to the touch when pressed by the finger. It if clings to the finger like the beaten white of the egg it needs longer in the oven. Fold and turn on hot platter, and pour around one and one half cups thing white sauce. Milk is sometimes used in place of hot water, but hot water leads to a more tender omelet.

Eggs a la Goldenrod

3 hardboiled eggs	1 tablespoon flour
½ teaspoon salt	5 slices toast
1 tablespoon butter	1 cup milk
¼ teaspoon pepper	Parsley

Make a thin white sauce with butter, flour, milk and seasonings. Separate yolks from whites of eggs. Chop whites firmly and add them to the sauce. Cut four slices of toast in halves lengthwise. Arrange on platter and pour over the sauce. Force the yolks through a potato ricer or strainer, sprinkling over the top. Garnish with parsley and remaining toast cut into points.

Many times eggs were used with other starches for meals other than breakfast. Often time's children would take fried egg sandwiches to school. The early pioneers used what they had in the way of food to make things stretch and do what they had to do to make

Grains and Cereals

In the days before there were raw cereals!!!
Cereals are the most important of the vegetable foods, for they contain in varying proportions all of the food principles. All are rich in starch, some have considerable amount of protein, some have fat, and all contain valuable mineral matter. Almost without exception, the cereals contain cellulose or tough woody fibers which form the framework of all vegetables and cereals. This cellulose requires long cooking to make it more digestible, therefore it follows that all cereals require careful cooking.

A double boiler is the best utensil for cooking cereals. The lower part should be filled one-third full of boiling water, the water should be kept boiling at all times and if necessary to replenish boiling water must be used. A double boiler may be improvised by placing one saucepan inside of a larger saucepan.

Stir the cereal gradually into the required amount of boiling salted water, place directly over the fire and cook form five to ten minutes, stirring to prevent burning. Place over the boiling water and cook the required time. Finely, ground cereals may be mixed with cold water before adding to the boiling water to prevent lumping.

Table for Cooking Cereals

Kind	Quantity	Water	Time
Steamed, cooked and rolled oats	1C.	2 C.	1 HR
Steamed, cooked and rolled wheat	1 C.	2 C.	¾ HR
Rice, steamed	1 C.	3 ½ C.	1 HR
Corn meal	1 C.	3 ½ C.	3 HR
Cream of wheat	1 C.	4 C.	1/2 HR
Coarse Oatmeal	1 C.	4 C.	5 HR
Hominy	1 C.	5 C.	5 HR

Add one teaspoon salt to each cup of cereal.

Boiled Rice

1 C. Rice
2 quarts boiling water
1 tablespoon salt

Pick over rice, add slowly to boiling salted water so as not to check boiling of water. Boil thirty minutes or until soft, which may be determined by testing kernels. Old rice absorbs much more water than new rice, and takes longer for cooking. Drain in coarse strainer and pour over one quart hot water; return to kettle in which it was cooked; cover, place on back of range, and let stand to dry off, when kernels are distinct. When stirring rice, always use a fork to avoid breaking kernels.

To wash rice: put rice in strainer, place strainer over bowl nearly full of water, rub rice between hands, lift strainer from bowl and change water. Repeat process three or four times until water is rain water clear.

Rice cooked in this way may be used with meats in place of potatoes, or may form the principal dish for supper or luncheon, serving with a tomato sauce and grated cheese which may be sprinkled over the top or served separately, so each person may use it or not.

Cheese sauce is also served with rice, this sauce is made by adding cheese in amounts according to taste, to white sauce.

Boiled Macaroni

¼ cup macaroni broken into pieces
2 quarts water
1 tablespoon salt

Cook macaroni in boiling salted water twenty minutes, or until soft, drain it in stranger, pour over it cold water to prevent pieces from sticking; reheat in the sauce in which it is to be served.

Fried Mush

Hominy cooked according to the same way as rice may also be served with cheese sauce. Cereals combined with these sauces, especially if cheese is used, make good meat substitutes.

Pick corn meal or hominy mush in greased, one pound baking powder cans or small bread pan, cool and cover. Cut into thin slices and sauté; cook slowly if desired dry and crisp. Serve with syrup.

If you use milk on your cereal remember to not let it sit around, but put in the well to keep cool. Letting milk sit increases the risk of sour milk.

Vegetables

Vegetables are particularly valuable for their mineral salts; some contain starch and some, as peas and beans, are rich in protein. This makes it possible to use them as meat substitutes; all vegetables contain a large amount of water.

Since all vegetables contain larges amount of cellulose (the woody framework) they must be cooked to make them tender. The succulent vegetables are those that contain a great deal of water. These vegetables are very poor in nutrients, but are valuable as a part of the diet in the summer, when the temperature of the body needs to be regulated.

Each vegetable contains a different mineral salt, so each should be eaten in its own season. All vegetables should be put into boiling water at first. Wilted vegetables should be soaked in cold water for several hours before cooking. Delicately flavored vegetables should be cooked at the simmering point. Strongly flavored vegetables should be cooked in large quantities of rapidly boiling water and uncovered. Starchy vegetables should be cooked at the boiling point until tender.

Salt toughens the cellulose, but it also intensifies the color of green vegetables; since they contain but a little cellulose it is well to use salt with them. While most of the vegetables have but little food value, if they are combined with milk, cheese, eggs, etc. they may form the principal part of a meal.

Asparagus

Boiled asparagus—cut off lower parts of stalks as far down as they will snap. Wash and remove scales. Cook in boiling water fifteen minutes or until soft, leaving tips out of water first ten minutes. Drain and spread with soft butter, allowing one and one-half tablespoons butter to each bunch of asparagus. Asparagus is often broken in inch pieces for boiling, cocking tips a shorter time than stalks. Serve boiled asparagus on buttered or milk toast. Boiled asparagus cut in one-inch pieces may be added to white sauce or cheese sauce, allowing one cup to each 2 Cups of asparagus.

Beans

String beans—remove strings, and snap or cut in one-inch pieces; wash and cook in boiling water from one to three hours, adding salt last half hour of cooking. Drain, season with butter and salt.

Baked Beans

Pick over one quart of beans, cover with cold water, and soak overnight. In the morning drain, cover with fresh water, heat slowly and cook until skins will burst which may be determined by taking a few beans on the top of a spoon and blowing on them – skins will burst if sufficiently cooked. Drain beans, scald rind of three-fourths pound of fat salt pork, scrape, remove one-fourth inch slice and put in bottom of bean pot. Cut through rind of remaining pork every half inch, cutting one inch deep. Put beans in pot and bury pork in beans, leaving rind exposed.

Mix one tablespoon salt, one tablespoon molasses, and three tablespoons sugar; add one cup boiling water and pour over beans; add enough more boiling water to cover beans. Put covered bean pot in oven and bake slowly six to eight hours, uncovering the last hour of cooking. Add water as needed.

Cream of Lima Beans

Soak one cup dried beans overnight, drain and cook in boiling salted water until soft; drain, add three-fourths cup cream, and season with butter and salt. Reheat before serving.

Boiled Beets

Wash and cook whole in boiling water until soft; time required being from one to four hours. Old beets will never be tender, no matter how long they may be cooked. Drain and put in cold water, that skins may be easily removed. Serve in quarters or slices.

Boiled Cabbage

Remove outer leaves, cut cabbage in quarters, and remove the tough stalks, soak in cold water, put into a large kettle nearly filled with rapidly boiling salted water, add one-fourth teaspoon of soda, cook twenty minutes uncovered, drain, re-cover with boiling water and cook till tender, drain and serve or cover with white sauce or drop and season with butter, salt and pepper. It may be put into a baking dish with layers of white sauce and or cheese sauce, covered with buttered crumbs and baked till brown.

Boiled Cream Corn

Remove husks and silky threads. Cook ten to twenty minutes in boiling water. Place on platter covered with napkin; draw corners of napkin over corn; or cut from cob and season with butter and salt.

Succotash

Cut hot boiled corn from cob, add equal quantity of hot boiled shell beans or stewed lima beans, season with butter and salt; reheat before serving.

Creamed Corn

2 tablespoons butter
2 tablespoons flour
½ green or red pepper
¼ tsp. salt
1 cup cow's milk

1 ½ cups green corn
1/3 cup bread crumbs
2 tablespoons melted butter

Make a sauce of the butter, flour and milk; add the corn and pepper, and turn into a buttered baking dish. Toss the bread crumbs in the melted butter. Spread over the corn. Bake until the crumbs are brown.

Carrots in Béchamel Sauce

Wash, scrape and cut carrots in thin strips about the size of a match and one-inch long, or in cubes; have about a quart when cut, cook in boiling salted water until tender, drain; reheat, add béchamel sauce.

Béchamel Sauce

Melt one tablespoon of butter and add one tablespoon of flour; when bubbling, stir in slowly one and one-half cupful's of milk, as for white sauce; when it has thickened, add the beaten yolks of two eggs, one-half teaspoon of salt, one-half teaspoon pepper, add the carrots and serve as soon as heated.

Celery in White Sauce

Wash, scrape and cut outer celery stalks in one-inch pieces; cook twenty minutes or until soft; in boiling salted water; drain and to two cups of celery add one cup of thin white sauce.

Fried Eggplant

Pare an eggplant and cut in thin slices. Dredge with flour and sauté slowly in butter until crisp and brown, or dip in flour eff and crumbs and fry in deep lard.

Boiled Onions

Put onions in cold water and remove the skins under water, put into saucepan of boiling salted water, boil five minutes, drain, cover again with boiling salted water, cook one hour or until soft, drain, add a small quantity of milk, cook for five minutes. Season to taste with butter, salt and pepper, or drain and partly cover with a thin white sauce.

Escalloped Onions
Cut boiled onions in quarters, put in a buttered baking dish, cover with white sauce, sprinkle with buttered crumbs and bake till brown.

Boiled Peas
Remove peas from pods, cover with cold water and let stand one-half hour. Skin off undeveloped peas which rise to top of water, and drain remaining peas. Cook until soft in a small quantity of boiling water, adding salt the last fifteen minutes of cooking. There should be but little, if any water, to drain from peas when they are cooked. Season with butter, salt and pepper. If peas have lost much of their natural sweetness, they are improved by the additional dash of sugar.

Creamed Peas
Drain boiled peas and to two cups peas add three-fourths cup of white sauce. Canned peas are often drained, rinsed and reheated in this way.

Stuffed Peppers
Cut a slice from the stem end of each pepper, remove the seeds, and parboil the pepper fifteen minutes. Fill with equal parts of finely chopped cooked chicken or veal and bread crumbs, tossed in a little melted butter and seasoned with onion juice, salt and pepper. Boiled rice may be used in places of the bread crumbs.

Glazed Sweet Potatoes

Wash and pare six medium sweet potatoes. Cook ten minutes in boiling salted water. Drain, cut in halves lengthwise, and put in a buttered pan. Make a syrup by boiling for three minutes one-half cup sugar and four tablespoons water, add one tablespoon butter. Brush potatoes with syrup and bake fifteen minutes, basting twice with remaining syrup.

Boiled Spinach

Remove roots, carefully pick over (discarding wilted leaves), and wash in several waters to be sure that it is free from all sand and dirt. When young and tender put in a stew pan and allow to heat gradually and cook twenty-five minutes, or until tender in its own juice. Old spinach is better cooked in boiling salted water, allowing two quarts of water to one peck spinach. Drain thoroughly, chop finely, reheat, and season with butter, salt and pepper. Garnish with slices of hardboiled eggs. The green color of spinach is better retained by cooking in a large quantity of water in an uncovered vessel.

Baked Winter Squash

Cut in pieces two inches square, remove seeds and stringy portion. Places in dripping pan, sprinkle with salt and pepper and allow for each square one-half teaspoonful molasses and one-half teaspoonful melted butter, keeping covered the first half hour of cooking. Serve in the shell.

Baked Tomatoes

Wipe and remove a thin slice from the stem end of six smooth, medium sized tomatoes. Take out seeds and pulp and drain off most of the liquid. Add an equal quantity of cracker and bread crumbs. Season with salt, pepper and a few drops of onion juice and refill tomatoes with the mixture. Place in a buttered pan, sprinkle with buttered crumbs and bake twenty minutes in a hot oven. Minced meat of any kind may be used with the crumbs and pulp.

Fried Tomatoes

Cut tomatoes in half-inch slices and season with salt and pepper, dip in beaten egg then in fine bread crumbs. Put some butter in a frying pan and brown the slices on both sides in the fat.

Turnips in White Sauce

Wash, pare and cut in cubes and cook until tender in boiling salted water, drain, reheat in white sauce and serve.

Potatoes

Baked Potatoes
Select potatoes of uniform size, wash, pare and put into cold water to prevent discoloration; cook in boiling salted water, one-half hour or till tender, allowing one teaspoonful of salt to every quart of water; drain well, put uncovered on back of stove and shake gently to let steam escape and make them mealy.

Mashed potatoes
Mashed potatoes in kettle in which they were boiled. To every pint of potatoes, add one tablespoon of butter, one-half teaspoonful salt, speck of pepper, and hot milk or cream to moisten. Beat until light and creamy, and pile lightly on a hot dish. Serve very hot.

Creamed Potatoes
Make one cupful of white sauce, cut one scant pint of cold boiled potatoes in dice, sprinkle lightly with salt, add to white sauce re-heating, sprinkle one tablespoonful of minced parsley over them and serve.

Escalloped Potatoes, No. 1
Wash, pare and slice raw potatoes, put a layer in a buttered baking dish, sprinkle with salt, pepper and flour, and one-half tablespoonful of butter, repeat: add hot milk till it may be seen through the top

layer, bake one and one-half hours or till potato is soft. Finely chopped red and green pepper and parsley give a delicious flavor to the potatoes.

Escalloped Potatoes, No. 2

Slice one quart of cold hardboiled potatoes, sprinkle lightly with salt and pepper, put a layer in a buttered baking dish, cover with a layer of white sauce, sprinkle with chopped parsley, repeat cover top with buttered crumbs, bake twenty minutes or until brown. If required one pint of sauce, one tablespoonful of minced onion or four hardboiled eggs, sliced may be added to the layer.

Lyonnaise Potatoes

One pint of cold boiled potatoes, one-half teaspoonful of salt, one-half salt, spoonful of dripping or lard, one tablespoon of chopped parsley. Cut potatoes into dice and season with salt and pepper, fry the onion in the dripping until a light brown, add potatoes, stir with a fork until they have absorbed the fat and are brown, add parsley and serve, one tablespoon of vinegar may be used.

Baked Potato

Select smooth potatoes of uniform size, wash and scrub well, bake in a hot pan for forty minutes or until soft, serve at once, uncovered, baked potatoes are more digestible than when cooked in any other way as the intense heat of the oven changes some of the starch to dextrin.

Potatoes Baked in Half-Shell

Select six medium sized potatoes and bake, following recipe for baked potatoes. Remove from oven, cut slice from tip of each and scoop out inside, mash, add two tablespoons butter, salt, pepper and three tablespoons hot milk' then ad whites of two eggs well beaten. Refill shells and bake five to eight minutes in very hot oven. Potatoes may be sprinkled with grated cheese before putting in oven.

Fried Potatoes

Wash and pare potatoes, slice thinly on a vegetable slicer into a bowl of ice water, let stand an hour, drain and dry between towels, fry in hot fat, stirring while frying to make them brown evenly; when a light brown, put in a colander, drain on brown paper, sprinkle lightly with salt.

French Fried Potatoes

Wash and pare potatoes, cut lengthwise and soak one hour in cold water, dry, and fry in hot fat, drain and sprinkle with salt.

Potato Croquettes

2 cups hot diced
potatoes
2 tablespoon butter
½ teaspoon salt
1/8 teaspoon pepper
¼ teaspoon celery salt

Dash cayenne pepper
Dash onion juice
1 egg yolk
1 teaspoon finely
chopped parsley

Mix ingredients in order given and beat thoroughly.
Shape, dip in crumbs, egg and crumbs again, fry
one minute in deep far, and drain on brown paper.
Croquettes are shaped in a variety of forms. The
most common way is to first form a smooth ball by
rolling one rounding teaspoon mixture between
hands. Then roll on a board until of desired length,
and flatten ends.

Sauces

Butter and flour are usually cooked together for thickening sauce, other fats may be used in place of butter. For brown sauces butter should be stirred until well browned, flour added and stirred with butter until both are browned, before liquid is added. The sauce of average thickness is made by allowing two tablespoons of each butter and flour to one cup of liquid. Milk, water, stock or strained tomato may be used as the liquid of a sauce.

Uses of Sauces

White sauce may be poured over toasted bread, with cold boiled or baked potatoes, with such vegetables as peas, beans, carrots, turnips, onion and asparagus. Cold chicken or veal cut in inch cubes, fish flaked in small pieces, codfish cooked until tender, or dried beef may be heated in the sauce, allowing about one cup of vegetable or meat for each cup of sauce.

Tomato sauce is suitable to serve with breaded veal, fish, boiled macaroni or rice.

Egg sauce is suitable to serve with fish, particularly with boiled or steamed fish.

White Sauce

2 tablespoons butter   ¼ teaspoon salt
1 cup milk   dash pepper
2 tablespoons flour

Put butter in saucepan, stir until melted and bubbling; add flour mixed with seasonings and stir until thoroughly blended. Pour on gradually the milk, adding about one-third at a time, stirring until well mixed, then beating until smooth and glossy.

Cheese Sauce

Add cheese to an ordinary white sauce, using from one to three-fourths a cup to each cup of sauce. This sauce is excellent with macaroni, rice, plain or in croquettes, and with vegetables, particularly asparagus, cauliflower, cabbage, and celery.

Brown Sauce

2 tablespoons butter   1 cup stock
½ slice onion   ¼ teaspoon salt
3 tablespoons flour   1/8 teaspoon pepper

Cook onion in butter until slightly browned; remove onion and stir butter constantly until well browned; add flour mixed with seasoning, and brown the butter and flour, then add stock gradually.

Tomato Sauce

2 tablespoons butter	½ teaspoon salt
2 tablespoons flour	1/8 teaspoon pepper
1 cup strained tomato	

Make in same manner as white sauce. Tomatoes are prepared by cooking with onion fifteen minutes then rubbing through strainer.

Drawn Butter Sauce

1/3 cup butter	½ teaspoon salt
3 tablespoons flour	1/8 teaspoon pepper
1 1/2 cup boiling water	

Melt one-half the butter, add flour with seasonings, and pour on gradually boiling water. Boil five minutes and add remaining butter.

Egg sauce

To drawn butter sauce, add two hard cooked eggs cut in one-fourth in slices

Meats

Roast Beef Gravy

Remove some of the fat from the pan, leaving thee tablespoonfuls. Place over fire, add three tablespoonfuls flour, and stir until well browned, add gradually one and one-half cups of boiling water, cook five minutes, season with salt and pepper and strain.

Beef Loaf

2 pounds lean beef	1/3 cup bread crumbs
½ tsp pepper	1 beaten egg
1 tablespoon finely	1 tsp. onion juice
chopped parsley	¼ teaspoon cayenne
¼ teaspoon mace	

Chop meat fine, add other ingredients, the egg beaten and the bread crumbs, wrung dry, after standing some time in cold water; mix thoroughly and shape into a roll. Bake in a small pan thirty or forty minutes. Baste frequently with fat from salt pork and water. Serve with brown or tomato sauce.

Beef Stew with Dumplings

Aitchbone weighting
5 lbs
½ of onion cut into
thin slices
4 cups potatoes cut in
¼ inch slices

¼ cup flour
2/3 diced turnips
2/3 cup diced carrot
Salt and pepper

Wipe meat, remove from bone, cut in one and one-half inch cubes, sprinkle with salt and pepper, and dredge with flour. Cut some of the fat in small pieces and try out in frying pan. Add meat and stir constantly; that the surface may be quickly seared; when well browned put in kettle, and rinse frying pan with boiling water, that none of the goodness may be lost. Add to meat remaining fat, and bone sawed in pieces; cover with salt and pepper the last hour of cooking. Parboil potatoes five minutes, and add to stew fifteen minutes before taking from fire. Remove bones, large pieces of fat, and then skim Thicken with ¼ cup flour, diluted with enough cold water to pour easily. Pour in deep hot platter and surround with dumplings. Remnants of roast beef are usually bade into beef stew; the meat having been once cooked, there is no necessity of browning it. If gravy is left, it should be added to the stew.

Broiled Beef Steak

Have five in readiness. Wipe meat, trim off any extra fat, grease a wire broiler with some of the fat and place meat in broiler and broil over a clear fire, turning it every time then is counted, until the surface is seared. Then turn occasionally until well cooked on both sides. Steak an inch thick require from five to eight minutes; an inch and a half thick require from eight to ten minutes. Remove steak to hot platter, spread with butter and sprinkle with salt and pepper. Put on warmer until ready to serve.

Pan Broiled Steak or Chops

Trim off all fat possible. Heat a frying pan very hot. Rub over lightly with a piece of fat. Lay in the meat, count ten slowly, then turn it. Count, and again turn and continue until the meat is cooked. If any fat collects while cooking, pour it off. To brown the fat of chops nicely without overcooking the meat, turn them up on the edge. Season and serve as broiled meats.

Broiled Meat Cakes

Chop finely lean, raw beef, season with salt and pepper, shape into small cakes, and broil in a greased broiler, or hot frying pan. Chopped onion or parsley may be added if desired, or they may be served with tomato sauce.

Veal Chops or Cutlets

Wipe, put on a rack in dripping pan, skin side down, rub over with salt, and dredge with flour. Place in a hot oven, that the surface may be quickly seared, thus preventing escape of juices. After flower is browned, reduce the heat and baste with fat which has tried out; if meat is quite lean it may be necessary to put trimmings of fat in pan. Baste every ten minutes. When meat is about half done, turn it over and dredge with flour, that skin side may be uppermost for final browning.

Dumplings

2 cups flour	½ teaspoon salt
4 teaspoons baking powder	2 teaspoons butter
	¼ cup milk

Mix and sift dry ingredients. Work in butter with tips of fingers, add milk gradually, using knife for mixing. Toss on a floured board, pat and roll out to one-half inch in thickness, shape with biscuit cutter first dipped in flour. Place closely together in a buttered steamer, put over kettle of boiling water, over closely, and steam twelve minutes. A perforated tin pie play may be used in place of a steamer. A little more milk may be used in the mixture, when it may be taken up by spoonfuls, dropped and cooked on top of stew. In this case some of the liquid must be removed, that dumplings may rest on meat and potatoes and not settle into liquid.

Roast Veal

When a leg of a veal is to be used, it should be boned. Wipe meat, sprinkle with salt and pepper, stuff and sew in shape. Place on rack in dripping pan, dredge meat and bottom of pan with flour and around the meat place strips of fat salt pork. Bake three or four hours in a moderate oven, basting every fifteen minutes with 1/3 cup of melted butter in ½ cup boiling water until used, then baste with the fat in the pan.

Swiss Steak

Three pounds of round steak cut one and one-half inches thick. Pound until fiber is thoroughly broken up, then pound into it tow large tablespoons of flour. Season with salt and pepper. Put two tablespoonfuls butter into a frying pan and brown the steak on both sides, then pour boiling water over it and let simmer until tender, about three hours.

Left-Over Meats

Scalloped meat

Chop any cold meat, mutton preferred, and put in bottom of baking dish; put over it a layer of boiled rice; pour over the whole a tomato sauce, letting it run through the rice and meat but do not stir them. Cover with buttered crumbs, place in a moderate oven and bake until crumbs are brown.

Scalloped Meats with a Twist

Cut cold meat into small pieces, season to taste and moisten with gravy. Make in layers with bread crumbs and bake twenty minutes in a hot oven or until the crumbs are brown.

Meat Timbales

3 cups cold finely
chopped meat
½ cup fine bread
crumbs
2 tablespoons butter
1 cup of stock or
goats milk

2 farm eggs
1 teaspoon parsley
½ teaspoon citrus
juice
Large dash of salt and
pepper

Mix seasonings and bread crumbs with the meat,
heat stock and melt the butter into it; then add the
stock and eggs, well beaten, to the meat. Mix
thoroughly and put in a well-buttered mold. Place in
pan of warm water and cover with a piece of
buttered paper, we use aluminum foil now. Cook for
an hour in a moderate oven, turn out on a platter and
pour brown or tomato sauce around it.

Meat and Potato Pie

Chop any cold meat or a mixture of meats, season
and moisten. Onion or parsley may be added. Place
meat in a baking dish and spread over the top a
layer of mashed potato. Smooth the potato and bake
from fifteen to thirty minutes or until a golden
brown.

Meat Balls

1 cup chopped meat	2 teaspoons gravy
2 teaspoons butter	2 teaspoons chopped
4 teaspoons flour	parsley
½ teaspoon salt	¼ teaspoon onion
2 eggs	juice

Mix all ingredients and shape into balls. Roll into crumbs, then in beaten egg, and again in crumbs, and fry in lard. Use one egg for mixture and the other for breading the balls.

Hash

To chopped meat add an equal quantity of cold boiled chopped potatoes. Season with salt and pepper, put into hot buttered frying pan, moisten with milk or cream, stir until well mixed, spread evenly, and then place where it may slowly brown underneath. Turn and fold, as an omelet, on a hot platter. Garnish with parsley.

Veal Croquette

2 cups chopped pre-cooked chilled veal	1/8 teaspoon pepper
	Dash onion juice
Dash cayenne	1 egg yolk
½ teaspoon salt	1 cup thick sauce

Mix ingredients in order given. In making the thick white sauce, use rich white stock in place of milk. Cook, shape, crumb, and fry same as other croquettes.

Fish

To Prepare Fish for Cooking

To clean: fish should be drawn immediately. Scrape the fish to remove the scales, beginning at the tail. Clean the fish to remove the scales; beginning at the tail. Clean the fish close to the backbone. Wash quickly, drain, and dry.

To Bone: begin at the tail on one side, slip knife between the flesh and bone and cut the flesh from the bone the entire length, holding the knife very closely to the bone. Remove the other side in the same manner. These pieces of fish may be cooked whole or cut into pieces of size suitable for serving. It is best to bone fish for all methods of cooking except baking.

Baked Fish

Clean, wipe, and dry fish. Do not remove the head and the tail. Rub all over with salt, stuff and sew up. Put two strips of cotton cloth in a pan, if you have not a fish sheet, to help remove the fish when baked. Lay the fish in a pan, and skewer into the shape of the letter S, cut gashes on top, and lay strips of salt pork in them and around the pan, sprinkle the fish with salt and pepper and dredge with flour; when the flour begins to brown baste with the fat in the pan. It is done when the fish separates easily from the bone. Lift carefully on a hot platter, draw the skewers or strings, and serve with drawn butter or egg sauce.

Stuffing for Fish

1 cup cracker crumbs	¼ teaspoon salt
¼ teaspoon pepper	1 teaspoon chopped onion
1 teaspoon chopped parsley	1 teaspoon chopped capers
1 teaspoon chopped pickles	1/3 cup melted butter

Toss the crumbs in the melted butter, add the other seasonings. This makes a dry, crumbly stuffing that is delicious with fish.

Fried Fish

Stream a whitefish till tender, remove bones and skin, and flake the fish, sprinkle with salt and pepper. Make a white sauce with one pint of milk, four tablespoons of flour and butter, add a dash of salt and pepper when cool add two beaten eggs, one tablespoonful each of minced onion and parsley. Put layers of fish and sauce in a baking dish, sprinkle top with buttered crumbs, and bake till golden brown.

Salmon in Mold

One fresh salmon, canned can be used, three eggs beaten lift, one-half cupful of fine bread crumbs, salt, cayenne, and parsley four tablespoon of melted butter. Remove oil, bones and skin from the fish, mince fish fine, rub in the butter till smooth, add crumbs to beaten eggs, season fish, add eggs and crumbs, put in a buttered mold and steam one hour. Serve with sauce.

Creamed Codfish

Pick salt codfish in small pieces, cover with cold water, heat and let simmer till tender, drain and cover with milk. When boiling, thicken with flour and butter rubbed together in the proportion of two tablespoonfuls of each to every cupful of milk. Just before serving add one beaten egg. Cook one minute.

Soups

Stock is the foundation of all meat soups and consists of the soluble parts of meat and vegetables dissolved out in water, with the addition of seasonings. To make soups, cut the meat in small pieces to expose all the surface possible, and put it into cold water, allowing it to stand or soak one-half hour before cooking it, this draws out all the juices. When cooking heat gradually, and simmer till the meat is in rags, the bones cleaned, and all the nutrients possible are extracted. This will take six to seven hours to do. The cheaper cuts of meat should be used for soups – the shin and rump bone of beef and the knuckle of veal. The water in which fresh meats are boiled may be boiled down, seasoned and used, in a large family all the leftovers may be added to the stock, and the trimmings and bones should always be sent from the butchers and thus and thus a palatable soup may be had at small expense.

The kettle should be of granite or porcelain lined or if not iron, should be very very smooth. The cover should fit closely to keep in all the steam. The scum which rises on the soup is the albumin and juices of the meat and should be removed if a clear soup is desired, but a clear soup is not the most nutritious. When the meat is in shreds the soup should be strained and allowed to cool, so that the fat may come to the surface in the form of a cake and be removed. A stock may then be reheated and served alone or with the addition of other ingredients. A brown soup may be made by browning part of the meat and vegetables before adding them to the stack. About two-thirds of the meat used should be lean, the other one-thirds of the meat used should be lean, the other one-third being bone and fat. Do not wash meat by putting into water to soak, but wipe thoroughly with a damp cloth before cutting.

Brown Soup Stock

6 lbs. shin of beef
3 quarts cold spring water
½ teaspoon peppercorns
6 cloves
¼ bay leaf
3 sprigs thyme

1 sprig marjoram
2 sprigs parsley
½ cup diced carrot
½ cup diced turnip
½ cup diced onion
½ cup diced celery
1 tablespoon salt

Clean beef, and cut the lean meat in inch cubes. Brown one-third of meat in hot frying pan in marrow from a marrow bone. Put remaining two-thirds with bone and fat in soup kettle, add water, and let stand for thirty minutes. Place on back of range, add browned meat, and heat gradually to boiling point during cooking. Add vegetables and seasonings, cook one and one-half hours, strain, and place in bowls, cool before serving.

Mixed Vegetable Soup

1 pint stock	¼ cup turnip
1 cup spring water	1 small onion
1 cup strained tomatoes	A dash of salt and pepper

Chop all vegetables fine and cook them in boiling salted water, add vegetables to stock and heat to boiling. Add pepper and place in bowls before serving.

Soups without Stock

Potato Soup

5 potatoes	¼ teaspoon celery salt
1 quart cow milk	¼ teaspoon pepper
2 slices of onion	Dash of cayenne pepper
2 tablespoons flour	
3 tablespoons butter	1 teaspoon chopped parsley
1 ½ teaspoon salt	

Cook potatoes in boiling salted water, when soft, rub through a strainer. Scald milk with onion, remove onion, and add milk slowly to potatoes. Melt half the butter, add dry ingredients, stir until well mixed, then stir into boiling soup: cook one minute, strain, add remaining butter, and sprinkle parsley.

Cream of Tomato Soup

1 pint tomatoes	1 slice onion
2 teaspoons sugar	¼ cup butter
¼ teaspoon soda	4 tablespoons flour
1 quart goat or cow's milk	1 teaspoon salt
	¼ teaspoon pepper

Scald milk with onion remove onion and thicken milk with flour diluted with cold water until thin enough to pour, being careful that the mixture is free from lumps: cook twenty minutes, stirring constantly at first. Cook tomatoes with sugar, can substitute honey, fifteen minutes, add soda, and rub through a sieve, combine mixtures, and strain into tureen over butter, salt and pepper.

Corn Soup

1 pint corn	2 tablespoons butter
1 pint boiling water	2 tablespoons flour
1 pint cow's milk	1 teaspoon salt
1 slice onion	Dash of pepper

Chop the corn, add water, and simmer twenty minutes; rub through a sieve. Scald milk with onion, remove onion, and add milk to corn. Bind with butter and flour cooked together. Add salt and pepper.

Salmon Soup

1 salmon from the river; gutted deboned and skinned	1 quart scalded milk
	1 ½ teaspoons salt
	2 tablespoons butter
4 tablespoons flour	Dash of pepper

Cook salmon in frying pan. Drain all fat, rub salmon through a sieve. Add gradually the milk, season and bind.

Celery Soup

3 cups celery (in ½ inch pieces)	2 ½ cups goat milk (can substitute cows)
1 slice onion	Dash of salt and
1 pint boiling water	pepper
¼ cup flour	

Wash and scrape celery before cutting into pieces, cook in boiling water until soft, rub through sieve. Scald milk with the onion, remove onion, and add milk to celery. Bind with butter and flour cooked together. Season with salt and pepper. Outer and old stalks of celery may be utilized for soups, great way to waste nothing.

Poultry

Dress and clean a chicken. Put stuffing by spoonfuls in the neck, using enough to fill the skin. Put remainder of stuffing in the body, and sew the skin.

Turn the third joints of the wings back over neck skin, turned down on the back and fasten with a skewer or by taking a stitch. Press the legs close to the body, drawing them as high as possible and hold by inserting a steel skewer under the middle joint, running it through the body. Cross drumsticks, tie securely with a long string, and fasten to tail. Draw string around each end of lower skewer; again cross string and draw around each end of upper skewer; fasten string and draw around each end of upper skewer; fasten string in a knot. Place on rack in dripping pan on its back. Spread slice of salt pork over the breast of chicken and place in a hot oven. Reduce the heat after fifteen minutes. Baste every ten minutes with fat from the pan or use ¼ cup butter melted in 2/3 cup boiling water. Dredge with flour after each basting. A four-pound chicken requires about 1 ½ hours, or until the joints separate easily. Pour off nearly all the fat, thicken the liquid in the pan with flour mixed in cold water, cook ten minutes, and add chopped giblets.

Bread Stuffing
To two cups of fine soft bread crumbs add two fresh
sage leaves, a sprig of summer savory, chopped
fine, teaspoon of onion juice, and half a teaspoon
salt mixed with ½ cup butter. Mix all together.

Maryland Chicken
Dress, clean and cut chicken in pieces suitable for
serving. Season with salt and pepper, and dip in
crumbs, egg and crumbs, place in a well-greased
dripping pan, and bake in a hot oven thirty minutes,
basting with 1/3 cup melted butter. Arrange on
platter and pour around its white sauce, over which
sprinkle chopped parsley. Old chicken should be
parboiled before breading and baking.

Cheese

Cheese is one of the most valuable of foods. Cheese is the solid part of milk, and is separated from the rest of the milk by rennin or lactic acid. This curd is subjected to a process of fermentation and ripening, seasoning and storage for varying periods of time, depending upon the particular kind of cheese being made. Cheese being so rich in casein may be substituted for meat, and as it is such a concentrated food, it is much more digestible when combined with other foods.

Cheese and Egg Sauce

2 cups grated or chopped cheese	2 eggs
1 cup dry bread crumbs	Dash of salt
Dash of cayenne	Dash of mustard
	1 cup milk

Melt the butter, add warm milk and bread crumbs, then the cheese, cook quickly; when cheese is melted add the egg beaten. If too thin, cook a little longer, if too thick, add a little milk. Consistency should be like pour batter. Serve on toast or heated crackers.

Welsh Rarebit

¼ cup grated cheese	1 egg
¼ cup milk or cream	1 teaspoon butter
½ teaspoon mustard	Speck cayenne
¼ teaspoon salt	Dry toast

Mix the mustard, salt and cayenne, add the egg and beat well. Stir in the milk, cheese and butter, pour into a double boiler and cook until the cheese is melted, stirring constantly, pour over the toast.

Cheese Custard

1 pint milk	1 ½ cups grated
2 eggs	cheese
½ teaspoon salt	1/8 teaspoon soda
1 pint bread crumbs	

Beat the eggs and mix with them the other ingredients, pour into buttered baking dish and bake in a moderate oven until brown on top.

Cheese Wafers

Sprinkle crisp crackers with grated cheese, mixed with a few grains of cayenne, lay them on a shallow pan, and bake until the cheese melt.

Cheese Soufflé

2 tablespoons of butter
3 tablespoons flour
½ cup scalded milk
½ teaspoon salt

Dash cayenne
¼ cup grated cheese
3 egg yolks
3 egg whites

Melt butter, add flour, and when well mixed add gradually scalded milk; then the seasonings and cheese. Remove from fire; add yolks of eggs beaten thoroughly. Cool the mixture and cut and fold whites of eggs beaten until stiff and dry. Pour into a buttered baking dish, and bake twenty minutes in a slow oven. Serve at once.

Cheese Balls

Chop one-half pound of good American cheese; add to it one pint of soft bread crumbs, a dash of cayenne pepper, 1 teaspoon of salt; mix and add two eggs unbeaten. From into balls the size of walnut. Dip into the beaten egg, then in crumbs, and fry in hot lard.

Salads

Cooked Salad Dressing

½ teaspoon salt	1 teaspoon mustard
1 ½ tablespoon sugar	Dash cayenne
½ teaspoon flour	2 egg yolks
1 ½ tablespoon melted butter	¼ cup vinegar

Mix dry ingredients, add yolks of eggs slightly beaten, butter, milk, and vinegar very slowly. Cook over boiling water until mixture thickens; strain and cool. A half cup of cream, whipped, may be added just before mixing the salad.

French Salad Dressing

One-half teaspoon of salt, one-fourth teaspoon pepper, two tablespoons of vinegar, four tablespoons of oil; mix ingredients and stir until well blended.

Mayonnaise Dressing

½ teaspoon mustard
Dash cayenne
½ teaspoon salt
1 egg yolk
½ tablespoon finely
grained brown sugar

1 tablespoon lemon
juice
1 tablespoon vinegar
1 cup oil

Mix dry ingredients, add egg yolk, beat until slightly thickened; add the lemon juice and vinegar, and beat thoroughly with an egg beater. Add the oil a teaspoonful at a time, beating while adding, and until it is toughly mixed. When about half of the oil is added, the remainder may be added by the tablespoonful. Mayonnaise should be stiff enough to hold its shape. It soon liquefies when added to meat or vegetables; therefore it should be added just before serving time.

Egg Salad

Hard cook eggs and place on lettuce leaves with dressing on top. Eggs may be sliced in rings or whites may be cut and arranged in any design and yolks may be forced through a strainer.

Lettuce Salad

Carefully wash and dry lettuce. Serve with French dressing.

Potato Salad

Cut cold boiled potatoes into half inch cubes, sprinkle lightly with salt, and add one-half the amount of celery, cut into cubes, a tablespoon of minced parsley, and a few drops of onion juice. Mix with a salad dressing and garnish with hard cooked eggs and parsley, the whites may be cut in rings and arranged about the base of the salad, and the yolks forced through a strainer and piled lightly over the top.

Cabbage Salad

Shred cabbage very fine, add half the quantity of celery, and one-fourth the quantity of almonds, blanched and cut lengthwise. Mix with the cooked salad dressing to which whipped cream has been added; serve on a large plate in cabbage leaves, placed to form a dish.

Salmon Salad

Drain oil from a can of salmon, remove bones and skin, flake the fish, mix with dressing, arrange on lettuce leaves. This salad may be varied by adding celery cut in diced or cucumbers cut in cubes, or a few cold cooked peas.

Chicken Salad

Cut cold boiled chicken into cubes, add an equal quantity of celery, washed and cut in cubes. Sprinkle lightly with cooked salad dressing. A few walnuts improve the salad. Remnants of other cold meats could be used in the same way, veal being particularly nice.

Tomato Salad

Peel medium-sized tomatoes. Remove thin slice from the top of each and take out seeds and some of the pulp. Sprinkle inside with salt, invert, and let stand one-half hour on ice. Fill tomatoes with the pulp that was removed, cut in small pieces, and mixed with cucumbers or celery, cut in cubes, all being mixed with boiled dressing Serve on lettuce or nasturtium leaves, and garnish the top of each with the dressing.

Quick Breads

Pop-Overs

1 cup flour
7/8 cup milk
¼ teaspoon salt

2 eggs
½ teaspoon melted butter

Mix salt and flour; add milk gradually, in order to obtain a smooth batter. Add egg beaten until light, and butter, beat two minutes using egg beater, turn into hissing hot buttered iron gem pans and bake thirty to thirty-five minutes in a hot oven. They may be baked in a buttered earthen cups, when the bottom will have glazed appearance. Small round iron gem pans are best for pop-overs.

Pop-overs may be filled with a thickened cream and used as a dessert, or apple sauce, jelly or fresh fruit may be used.

Cream Filling

1 cup milk
2 tablespoons sugar
1 tablespoon cornstarch

1 egg
1/8 teaspoon salt
¼ teaspoon vanilla

Blend the cornstarch in a little cold water and add to milk in a double boiler, stirring constantly until thickened, then occasionally for ten minutes. Beat the egg and sugar and salt, then pour on it a little of the thickened milk, then add to remainder of milk in double boiler and cook for a few minutes. When cooled add the vanilla; make an opening in the popover and put in the cream.

Sweet Milk Griddle Cakes

3 cups flour
1 ½ tsps. Baking powder
1 egg

1 teaspoon salt
¼ cup sugar
2 cups milk
1 tbsp melted butter

Mix and sift dry ingredients, beat egg, add milk and pour slowly over first mixture. Beat thoroughly and add butter. Cook as sour milk griddle cakes.

Muffins

2 cups flour
4 tsp. baking powder
1 egg
2 tablespoons sugar

1 cup milk
½ teaspoons salt
2 tbsp melted butter

Mix and sift dry ingredients, add gradually milk, egg well beaten and melted butter. Bake in buttered gem pans about 25 minutes.

Graham Muffins

Substitute one cup of graham flour in place of one of the cups of white flour in the Muffins recipe. Entire wheat flour and corn meal may also be substituted in the same way.

Corn Griddle Cakes

2 cups flour	1/3 cup sugar
½ cup corn meal	1 ½ cups boiling
1 ½ tbsp. baking	water
powder	2 tbsp. melted butter
1 egg	1 ½ tsp salt

Add meal to the boiling water, and boil five minutes; turn into a bowl, add milk and remaining dry ingredients mixed and sifted, then the egg well beaten, and butter. Cook as other griddle cakes.

Buckwheat Cakes

1 cup rye meal	¾ tablespoon baking
1 cup corn meal	soda
¼ cup molasses	1 teaspoon salt
2 cups sour milk or 1	1 cup graham flour
¾ cups sweet milk or	
water	

Mix all the ingredients together and beat thoroughly. Let rise over night in a warm place. In the morning add one-fourth teaspoon of soda and one tablespoon of sugar. One tablespoon of butter added to the mixture will prevent the cakes from sticking without the use of fat on the griddle, if the griddle is just the right temperature.

Boston Brown Bread

1 cup rye meal
1 cup corn meal
¼ cup molasses
2 cups sour milk or 1
¾ cups sweet milk or
water

¾ tablespoon baking
soda
1 teaspoon salt
1 cup graham flour

Mix and sift dry ingredients, add molasses and milk, stir until well mixed, turn into a well buttered mold and steam three and one-half hours. The cover should be buttered before being placed on mold. Mold should never be filled more than two-thirds full. A melon mold or one-pound baking powder boxes make the most attractive shaped loaves, but a five-pound lard pail answers the purpose. For steaming, place mold on a trivet in kettle containing boiling water, allowing water to come half way up around mold, cover closely, and steam adding as needed more boiling water.

Dutch Apple Cake

1 pint flour
1 egg
¼ tsp. salt
1 scant cup milk

4 sour apples
4 tsps. baking powder
2 tbsp. sugar

Mix dry ingredients in the or given, rub in the butter; beat the egg and mix it with the milk; then stir this into the dry mixture. The dough should be soft enough to spread half an inch thick on a shallow baking pan. Core, pare and cur four or five apples into eights; lay them in a parallel row on top of the dough, the sharp edge down, and press enough to make the edge penetrate slightly. Sprinkle the sugar on the apple. Bake in a hot oven twenty or thirty minutes, to be eaten hot with butter as a tea cake or with lemon sauce as a pudding.

Strawberry Short Cake

2 cups flour
¼ cup sugar
4 tablespoons baking powder
1/3 cup milk butter

Dash nutmeg
1 egg
1/3 cup butter
½ teaspoon salt

Mix and sift together dry ingredients, work in the butter, add egg, well beaten, and enough of the milk to make a soft dough. Toss on a floured board, pat, roll out rather thin, and cut with a biscuit cutter. Place in a pan, brush over with melted butter, and place a second biscuit on top (baked in this way they separate easily without cutting). Bake about twelve minutes in a hot oven. When baked break apart and put between and on top strawberries, crushed and sweetened to taste. Whipped cream may be used as a garnish, and whole berries placed on top of cream. Other berries, peaches, oranges, and bananas may be used.

Baking Powder Biscuit

1 C. flour
1 Tbsp. lard
4 tsp. baking powder

¾ cup milk and water in equal parts
1 tbsp. butter
1tsp. salt

Mix dry ingredients and sift twice. Work in butter and lard with tips of fingers; add gradually the liquid, mixing with knife to soft dough. It is impossible to determine the exact amount of liquid, owing to differences in flour. Toss on a floured board, pat, and roll lightly to one-half inch in thickness. Shape with a biscuit cutter. Place on buttered pan and bake in hot oven twelve to fifteen minutes.

Apple Dumplings

Pare and core six sour apples; fill the centers with sugar and a little cinnamon. Use recipe for biscuits, divide the dough in a six pieces, roll out each piece separately, put an apple in the center and press the edges of the dough together. Place on a greased pan and bake in a hot oven about thirty minutes; or place in a steamer and steam from forty-five minutes to one hour. Serve with lemon sauce or with sugar and cream.

Fruit Rolls

Use baking powder biscuit dough, or a richer dough if desired; roll thin, spread with a mixture of chopped figs, raisins and nuts, or shopped cooked prunes alone may be used; roll up like a jelly roll, cut into inch pieces and bake in a quick oven. These rolls may be used as a tea biscuit or a sauce may be served with them and used as a dessert.

Breads

In all mixtures in which yeast is used to leaven, bread flour should be used. Wheat and rye are the only two grains that contain gluten of a good quality and of sufficient quantity to make a good loaf of bread. This gluten when separated from the rest of the flour is a grayish yellow, tenacious, elastic mass and it is the elasticity which makes it so valuable in bread making, for as the gas is formed during the process of fermentation, it stretches, thus holding the gas in. The best bread is made from the white wheat flour, and the best bread flour is made from the spring wheat, for it contains more gluten than does the winter wheat.

Good bread flour is granular and easily slips through the sieve, while the pastry flour is more solid. It also is of a creamy color.

Bread is baked:
1. To kill the ferment
2. To make the starch soluble
3. To drive off the alcoholic and carbonic acid gas
4. To form a brown crust of pleasant flavor

Liquid, dry, or compressed yeast may be used in bread making. The latter makes excellent bread when it can be obtained perfectly fresh. The yeast plant is killed when heated to 212 degrees F; life suspended, but not utterly destroyed at 32 degrees

F. The best temperature for its growth is 75 to 80 degrees F. Yeas is a microscopic plant of fungus growth which multiplies very rapidly under favorable conditions, and by this process of growing causes a chemical change called fermentation. Alcoholic fermentation is that which is produced in substances rich in sugar and starch. Under the influence of warmth and moisture and some ferment (yeast) the starch is converted into sugar and the sugar into alcohol and carbonic acid gas. This is the fermentation that takes place in bread making; the carbonic acid gas seeking to escape lightens the dough, if alcoholic fermentation goes beyond a certain limit, acetic fermentation takes place, in which the alcohol formed is turned into acetic acid and the mixture is sour.

The Baking of Bread
The oven should be hot enough to turn a piece of white paper a dark brown in five minutes for the baking of bread. (If we did that today we would be risking the insurance wrath, when things went wrong). The heat should increase slightly for the first ten minutes and gradually decreased till the end of the baking. The heat in the center of the loach should reach 212 degrees F, or otherwise the starch grains will not be ruptured or the yeast plants killed. The heat changes the starch on the exterior of the loaf to dextrin, when the loaf is removed from the oven; place it where the air will circulate freely around it. Do not cover if you like crisp crust. When cold, put it into a clean bread box, without any wrapping, as the latter will give it a musty flavor.

Another tip for bread is when the bread has 3 more minutes to cook carefully rub butter of the top of the bread and then continue baking.

The pan for baking bread should not be over four inches wide, four inches deep, and suited in length to the oven. When the loaf is larger than this, there is danger of the temperature in the center of the loaf not to reach 212 degrees F, and the yeast not being killed. When you hear of bread baking day you know why know as it took a whole day to get all the bread baked that was needed for one week. Some women baked more than 7 loaves of bread in one day just to keep up with the demands of their family.

Bread is made by mixing to a dough flour with a definite quantity of milk or water, salt, and ferment. Enough sugar should be added to restore the natural sugar of the wheat changed during fermentation. The dough is then kneaded to thoroughly incorporate the ingredients, and is allowed to rise till double in bulk. It is then kneaded a second time to break the large bubbles of gas formed. It is shaped into loaves and allowed to rise again, if it rises too long it will be coarse grained; if not long enough, it will be heavy.

Raw Potato Yeast

One-fourth cup of flour, one-fourth cup of sugar, one tablespoon of salt, three raw potatoes, one to two quarts of boiling water, one cupful or one cake compressed yeast. Pare potatoes and keep in cold water, mix flour, sugar and salt in a large bowl, and grate the potatoes in as quickly as possible, mix at once with a wooden spoon, pour the boiling water directly from the teakettle over the, stirring constantly, and adding enough water to make it the consistency of thin starch; if compressed, dissolve in one cupful of water, keep mixture in a warm (not hot) place till light, beat well several times at the end of twenty-four hours, put in earthen or glass jars, cover tightly and put in a cool place. This will keep for two weeks.

If liquid yeast is used, allow one-half cup to one pint of liquid.

Yeast Starter

Take 1 cup of the mixture above and put with 1 cup flour and 1 cup sugar, and one cup liquid, either mil or water, stir in glass container and with wooden spoon. This mixture will serve as yeast. Use 1 cup for a cake of yeast. Keep in a non-drafty place with a towel over it. Stir and add to when you use the mixture again.

Swedish Rolls

1 pint scalded milk	2 egg whites
½ cup butter	¼ cup sugar
1 yeast cake dissolved	1 teaspoon salt
in ¼ cup lukewarm	Flour (probably 2-4
water	cups)
¼ cup sugar	

Pour hot milk over the sugar, salt and butter; when lukewarm add the yeast and beaten whites of eggs. Add enough flour to make a sponge. When light, add enough more flour to knead. Knead and let rise to double its bulk, then knead again slightly, and roll out into a rectangular piece, half an inch thick, having the edges as straight as possible. Spread all over with soft butter and sprinkle with sugar, cinnamon, grated lemon rind, and currants. Roll up like a jelly roll, cut off slices an inch wide, lay them with the cut side down on well-greased pans, and when lift bake in a hot oven fifteen or twenty minutes. When nearly done, glaze them by using a little cold water, pour on three-fourths cup of boiling water and let simmer ten minutes. Brush over the top with the starch and dredge with sugar.

Butter on bread was a treat for most. Most settlers ate a slice of bread plain. When butter was used many wanted to save it: to save butter take 2 pints sweet milk, ½ crock butter. Allow butter to remain out until very soft. Heat ½ of milk fairly hot. Mix with softened butter and beat with egg beater or place back in churn and churn until thick. Then add other half of cold milk. Finish churning or beating until thick again. Then place back in cool place.

Entire Wheat Bread

2 cups scalded milk
1 teaspoon salt
2 ¾ cups white flour
¼ yeast cake
dissolved in ¼ cup
lukewarm water

¼ cup sugar or 1/3
cup molasses
3 ¼ cups entire wheat

Put butter, lard, sugar and salt in bread raiser, or large bowl; pour on boiling water, when lukewarm add dissolved yeast cake and five cups of flour; then stir until thoroughly mixed, using a knife or mixing spoon. Add remaining flour mix and turn on a floured board, leaving clean bowl; knead until mixture is smooth, elastic to touch, and bubbles may be seen under the surface. Some practice is required to knead quickly, but the motion once acquired will never be forgotten. Return to bowl, cover with a clean cloth kept for the purpose, and board or tin cover. Let rise until double its bulk (it usually requires about two hours). Toss on board slightly floured, knead, shape into laves or biscuits, place in greased pans, having pans nearly half full. Cover, let rise again to double its bulk, and bake in hot oven. This recipe will make a double loaf of bread and pan of biscuits. Cottolene, cottosuet or beef drippings may be used for shortening, one-third less being required. Bread shortened with butter has good flavor but is not as white as when lard is used. Use one-fourth yeast cake if bread is to be started at night. When one yeast cake is used, bread may be made in five hours. Heating milk is inclined to stick at the bottom of the pan. Use lard and grease the pan before boiling the milk.

Graham Bread

2 ½ cups hot water or milk
¼ yeast cake dissolved in ¼ cup lukewarm water

½ cup molasses
3 cups flour
1 ½ teaspoons salt
3 cups graham flour

Prepare just like entire wheat bread. The bran remaining in sieve after sifting graham flour should be discarded.

Cakes

Tips for Cakes:

To Mix Sponge Cake

Separate the yolks from the whites, beat the yolks till lemon colored and thick, add the sugar gradually, and stiff, sift in the flour carefully, and do not beat after adding the flour, or air bubbles will be broken and the cake will be coarse grained and tough.

To Mix Butter Cakes

Use an earthen bowl and wooden spoon. Have all the ingredients measure and ready, the pans greased before beginning to mix the cake. Cream the butter, add the sugar gradually, and beat till very light; add the beaten yolks, flavoring, then the milk, and the flour in which the baking powder has been sifted, alternately; then fold in the beaten whites. Never stir the cake after the final beating.

Putting into the Pans

Line the tines with paper grease with lard or clarified butter, dredge the pan with flour, shake it all out, leaving only what clings to the lard, fill the pans about two-thirds full, having the mixture come well in the corners, and leave a slight depression in the middle, so that the cakes will be level when baked.

Baking

The baking is the most critical part of cake making. Test the oven with a piece of white paper. If it turns a light yellow in five minutes, it is ready for sponge cake; it a dark yellow in five minutes it is ready for cupcakes. The time of baking should be divided into quarters. During the first quarter the mixture should begin to rise; during the second quarter it should continue to rise and begin to brown; in the third quarter continue browning; in the last quarter finish baking and shrink from the edge of the pan. Cake should not be moved until it has risen its full height. When it feels firm to the touch, shrinks from the pan, a straw of hay inserted will come out clean, and it stops cracking, a cake is done. Small and layer cakes require a hotter oven than sponge and loaf cakes.

Sour Cream Cakes

2 eggs
1 ½ cups flour
1 C. brown sugar
1 tsp. salt

1 cups sour cream
2 tsps. Soda dissolved in water

Beat the eggs, add the sugar, and cream, then the soda dissolved in water, and last the flour mixed with the salt. Bake in small pans. Flavoring may used, or spices may be sifted in the flour.

Note: Sour cream is not like the kind that we buy at the stores now days to put on baked potatoes. It was cream that was skimmed off the daily cows or goats milk after milking. It if became sour this is when cakes and other goodies were baked. Because there were not great lots nothing was wasted.

Sponge Cake

6 egg yolks
½ of a lemon rind grate
1 cup sugar

6 egg whites
¼ tsp. salt
1 tbsp. lemon juice
1 cup flour

Beat yolks until tick and lemon colored, add sugar gradually, and continue beating, using egg beater. Add lemon juice, rind, and white of eggs beaten until stiff and dry. When whites are partially mixed with yolks, remove beater and carefully cut and fold in flour mixed and sifted with salt. Bake one hour in a slow oven, in a deep narrow pan.

Butter Cake

½ cup butter
2 cups sugar
4 eggs
1 teaspoon flavoring
1 cup milk

3 cups flour
2 teaspoons baking
powder
1 salt spoon mace

Cream the butter, add one cup of sugar, add the remaining cup of sugar to the beaten egg yolks, beat until very light, and add to the butter. Add flavoring. Beat the whites stiff and dry, add milk and flour mixed with baking powder, alternately to the mixture. Add whites of eggs. Bake in a moderate oven until the loaf shrinks from the pan.

Angel Cake

1 cup egg whites
1 cup sugar
½ teaspoon cream of
tartar

1 tsp. vanilla
flavoring
1 cup flour

Beat whites of eggs until foamy, add cream of tartar and beat until dry; beat in sugar gradually using spoon; add the extract, fold in the flour; bake in a deep pan, unbuttered. This cake requires from thirty to fifty minutes, according to the depth of the pan.

White Cake

½ cup butter
1 ½ cup sugar
2 ½ cup flour
2 tsp. baking powder

½ cup milk
½ tsp almond flavoring
5 egg whites

Follow directions according to the butter cake and bake in a shallow pan.

Chocolate Cake

½ cup butter
2 ½ teaspoons baking powder
2 ounces chocolate

1 ¾ cup flour
1 ½ cup sugar
½ cup milk
5 tablespoons water

Cream the butter, add sugar gradually, and then yolks of eggs, beaten thoroughly. Sift flour and baking powder together, and add alternately with the milk to the creamed mixture, add the chocolate melted in the water and lastly the stiffly beaten egg whites. Bake in layer cake pans and put layers together with frosting. (Make sure to cool the cakes thoroughly before frosting to avoid crumbs in the frosting.)

Spice Cake

½ cup butter	1 tsp soda
1 ½ cups brown sugar	1 cup sour milk
1 tsp cinnamon	1 cup raisins
½ cup currants	1 tsp cloves
3 cups flour	¼ tsp. ground nutmeg

Follow directions according to the butter cake and bake in a shallow pan. This cake is economical and improves by keeping.

Plain Cake

2 eggs	1 cup sugar
1 ½ cups flour	1 tablespoon melted
3 teaspoons baking	butter
powder	½ teaspoon flavoring
½ cup milk	

Mix in order given and put together quickly. Bake in layer cake pans and use any desired filling.

Gingerbread

¼ cup butter	½ cup sour milk
½ tsp. soda	½ cup sugar
½ tsp cinnamon	1 egg
1 ¾ cup flour	½ cup molasses
1 tbsp ginger	1 tsp. salt

Cream the butter, add the sugar gradually. Mix and sift together dry ingredients. Mix together liquid ingredients and add alternately with dry ingredients to the creamed mixture.

Nut Cake

½ cup butter
1 cup nuts
1 cup sugar
4 tbsp milk

3 eggs
1 ½ cups flour
2 teaspoons baking powder

Mix in order given and put together quickly. Bake in small pans.

Cookies

Imperial Cookies

½ cup butter
1 cup sugar
2 eggs
1 tablespoon milk
2 ½ cups flour

2 teaspoons baking powder
½ teaspoon flavoring
½ teaspoon grated nutmeg

Cream the butter, add sugar, egg well beaten, milk, and flavoring. Mix and sift dry ingredients and add to first mixture. Chill thoroughly. Toss one-fourth of mixture on a floured board and roll as thinly as possible; shape with a small round cutter, first dipped in flour. Placed near together on a buttered sheet and bake in a moderate oven. Gather up the trimmings and roll with another portion of dough, during rolling the bowl containing the mixture should be kept in a cool place, or it will be necessary to add more flour to dough, which makes cookies hard rather than crisp and short.

Ginger Snaps

1 cup molasses
½ cup shortening
3 ¼ cup flour

½ teaspoon soda
1 tablespoon ginger
1 ½ teaspoon salt

Heat molasses to boiling point and pour over shortening. Add dry ingredients mixed and sifted. Chill thoroughly. Proceed as in imperial cookies.

Hermits

1/3 cup butter
2/3 cup sugar
1 egg
2 tablespoons milk
¼ teaspoon mace
2 tablespoons baking powder
½ cup raisins chopped
½ teaspoon cinnamon
¼ teaspoon cloves
1 ¾ cup flour
¼ teaspoon nutmeg

Cream the butter, add sugar gradually, the raisins, egg well beaten, and milk. Mix and sift dry ingredients and add to first mixture. Roll mixture a little thicker than for imperial cookies.

Odds and Ends

Feed and Sugar Sack Lettering Removal

To remove the lettering from feed and sugar sacks soak them in a solution of kerosene and salt. Roll up wet and let stand all night. Was as usual and lettering will vanish.

Feed sacks can still be purchased online for your use. They are high dollar at this point but you can still find them.

I remember as a child we used them as tea towels. Mother and my Mother in law talked about feed sack dresses and I still have fabric that was feed sacks.

Face Powder

10 cents worth flakes white
1 cent worth lard
1 cent worth rose water

Put above into a pint jar and fill 2/3 full of rain water. We have laughed for years at this. Still have not found anyone who knows what flakes white is.

Soap

Use any old kind of lard or fat, 1 cup warm fat, 2 cup boiled hot water, 3 tablespoons of lye. Use a large cup for measuring. Put lye in a large crock. Pour hot water in very slowly stirring all the time to mix well. Let stand for 3 or 4 minutes, then pour in the warm fat very slowly, stirring all the time. Beat with an eff beater, about twenty minutes, until the crock is cold and the soap is thick. Pour in muffin tins. Cover well and let stand 24 hours. Put on cloth or board to dry a week, turning daily or more often if humid. Never use over 2 cups of fat at a time for best results. Sometimes water forms at the bottom of the pan, just pour off and it will not hurt the soap.

Washing white collars
To wash a white collar which is sewed to a colored dress, pin a towel around the neck of the dress leaving the collar to be washed. By being careful it can be easily washed without getting the dress wet.

When Making Pillows
When making pillows, make a slip of fine netting and put the feathers into this; slip this into the ticking. It will be much easier to remove when airing the ticking and pillow out for washing.

Making Mops
When men's old socks become worn cut from the top to the toe and put several socks together on your mop. This makes a good soft mop.

White Wash
Whitewash that will not flake off! Use one half gallon sweet skim milk, 2 quarts air-slacked lime, 1 pint salt, and 1 pint flour. Add water enough to make a thick paste or whitewash. Beat and stir until smooth. This will give three years wear without flaking.